Integrated Chinese
中文听说读写

Simplified Character Edition
Character Workbook

Tao-Chung Yao, Yuehua Liu
Xiaojun Wang, Yea-fen Chen, Liangyan Ge
with Jeffrey J. Hayden

Cheng & Tsui Company

First edition 1997
2003 Printing

Cheng & Tsui Company
25 West Street
Joston, MA 02111-1213 USA

Simplified Character Edition
ISBN 0-88727-267-3

Companion textbooks, workbooks and audio tapes are also available from the publisher.

Printed in the United States of America

PUBLISHER'S NOTE

The Cheng & Tsui Company is pleased to announce the most recent addition to its Asian Language Series, *Integrated Chinese*. This entirely new course program for the beginning to advanced student of Mandarin Chinese will incorporate textbooks, workbooks, character workbooks, teaching aids, audio tapes, video tapes, CD-ROM computer programs and interactive multimedia programs. Field-tested since 1994, this series has been very well received. It is our intention to keep it a dynamic product by continuing to add, revise and refine the content as we get your valuable feedback.

This series seeks to train students in all four language skills: listening, speaking, reading and writing. It utilizes a variety of pedagogical approaches—grammar translation, audio-lingual, direct method, total physical response—to achieve the desired results. Because no two Chinese language programs are the same, *Integrated Chinese* provides those classes that cover the lessons more speedily with additional material in the form of Supplementary Vocabulary. The Supplementary Vocabulary section, however, is purely optional.

The *C&T Asian Language Series* is designed to publish and widely distribute quality language texts as they are completed by such leading institutions as the Beijing Language Institute, as well as other significant works in the field of Asian languages developed in the United States and elsewhere.

We welcome readers' comments and suggestions concerning the publications in this series. Please contact the following members of the Editorial Board:

Table of Contents

Preface

This *Character Workbook* is a companion volume to *Integrated Chinese, Textbook, Level I, Part 1 (Simplified Character Version)*. *Integrated Chinese* is a series of Chinese language textbooks written by the *Integrated Chinese* committee which consistes of seven members (Nyan-ping Bi, Yea-fen Chen, Liangyan Ge, Yuehua Liu, Yaohua Shi, Xiaojun Wang, and Tao-chung Yao). The first two levels of *Integrated Chinese* are available now. In addition to this *Character Workbook*, there is another workbook for students to learn the four language skills (listening, speaking, reading, and writing).

This book is designed to help the student to learn Chinese characters in their correct stroke order, and then by components. We believe that the student will learn a new character more easily if he/she can identify the components in each character and know why the specific components are used in each character. Therefore we strongly urge teachers to teach their students the 40 basic radicals which are frequently used to compose Chinese characters.

When learning a new character, the first thing that the student should do is to try to identify the known component(s). By doing that, the student will only need to remember what components are in the character, rather than remember the composition of many meaningless strokes. For example, both 女 (nǚ, female) and 马 (mǎ, horse) are taught in the radical section. When the student sees the character 妈 (mā, mother) in Lesson 2, he/she should be able to tell that the new character 妈 consists of two known components, namely, 女 and 马. The components in a character sometimes give clues to the meaning and pronunciation of the character. The radical 女 in the character 妈 suggests that the character might be related to females and the other component, 马, is a phonetic element giving a clue to its pronunciation. If a student can remember that the character for "mother" sounds like "horse", he/she would have an easier time learning how to write the character. It would be a very painful way to learn the character 妈 if all one sees is a character consisting of a number of meaningless strokes, with a few vertical lines, a few horizontal lines, a few dots, etc.

The 40 radicals selected here, of course, are just some of the components that are seen in Chinese characters. However, by mastering these 40 radicals the student will realize that many characters contain one or two of the 40 components, and that the student only need to concentrate on the new components which he/she has not seen before. By knowing the meanings and the pronunciations of the components of the new character, the student will be able to retain the shape and the sound of the new character better.

After the radicals section in this workbook there is a small section for numerals. Since numerals are extremely useful in everyday life, we urge students to learn the characters 1-10 as soon as possible. Also, these characters are quite easy to write and can serve as a good introductory lesson for beginning students.

Each page of this *Character Workbook* has three to four new characters on it. Each new character is displayed in a large point size on the left side of the page, with its *pinyin* reading and English translation immediately to the right. Next to the *pinyin* reading there is a number in parentheses. The number indicates the ranking of the character given in the <u>Xiàndài Hànyǔ Pínlù Cídiǎn</u> (《现代汉语频率词典》, *The Dictionary of Modern Chinese Word Frequency*). For example, for the character 人 (rén, person), the number "9" given in the parentheses means that this character is the ninth most frequently used character in the Chinese language.

The symbol "†" in the parentheses indicates that the character does not belong to the 1000 most frequently used characters according to the <u>Xiàndài Hànyǔ Pínlù Dà Cídiǎn</u>. While we try to introduce the first 1000 most frequently used characters in the first two levels of *Integrated Chinese*, we sometimes have to include some characters beyond the first thousand to make the text natural and functional.

In the radical section, under the English translation of the radical, a smaller size of the same character is found. If the radical has a variation, then the variation is given to the right side of the smaller character. Both the radical and its variation will have pen versions below them. If a radical has a traditional form, it is also given to the right side of the smaller character, but there is no pen version for it. In the main lessons, the traditional version of the character is given to the right of the smaller simplified character. Occasionally the traditional character to the right will have the small symbol "Δ" after it indicating the printing form. Each practicing unit for a character contains three or four rows of small boxes. The first row has a grayed version of the character. The student is expected to trace this. The second row is in graph-style layout to facilitate practice at character proportion. The third row and the remaining empty boxes are for the student to practice writing the character. By this time, the student can be expected to be able to draw the character in proper spatial proportions without the use of any guides.

It is very important that each character is drawn in the correct stroke order. Two devices are used in this workbook to show a character's stroke order. The small numbers printed along the large characters indicate the sequence of the strokes. In general, every effort has been made to place the number at the starting point of the stroke. Because in some instances it is not very easy to tell which number goes with what stroke, or to tell where each stroke begins and ends, a "pen version" of each character is provided. Right below the large character, the character is drawn one step at a time to show

how it is formed. Students should consult with this series of strokes when practicing writing characters.

For components which have previously appeared, the pen version may simply show the entire component already drawn rather than writing it out one stroke at a time. For example, the pen version for the character 明 (míng, bright) in Lesson 4 only uses two boxes, one for 日, and one for 明. This means that when writing the character 明, one first writes 日, and then one writes 月 next to 日 to form 明. No individual strokes are given here because the student has already learned how to write 日, and 月 separately.

There are many computer programs (such as *Chinese Character Tutor* by Ted Yao and Mark Peterson and *Hanzi Assistant* by Panda Software) which are designed to teach stroke order. Students are encouraged to use them if they have access to the software. For more information on computer software for learning Chinese characters, please see our home page at <http://www.lll.hawaii.edu/ICUsers/>.

The three people who have spent the most time in preparing this *Character Workbook* are Tao-chung Yao, Jeffrey J. Hayden, and Xiaojun Wang. Yao designed the format for the first two versions (1994, 1995) and wrote the stroke numbers by hand. Wang did the calligraphy for the very first version (1994) and has also done most of the the pen version stroke ordering in this current edition. Yao and Hayden collaborated on the 1996 and 1997 editions. Yao has been responsible for the overall planning, and Hayden has translated Yao's ideas into the current form, including entering all of the data and numbering each stroke. We would like to thank Mr. Song Jiang for doing the pen version stroke ordering for many characters in this volume on such short notice.

RADICALS AND NUMERALS

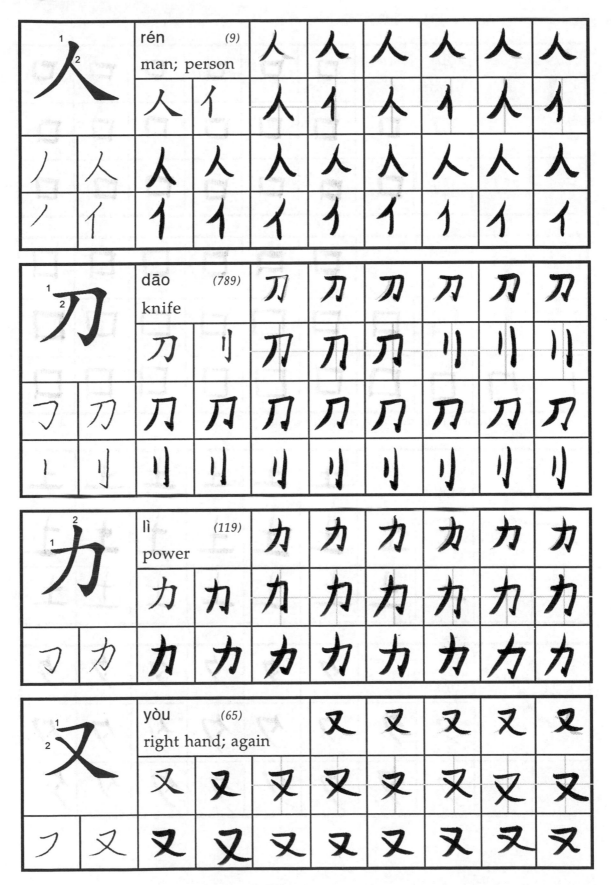

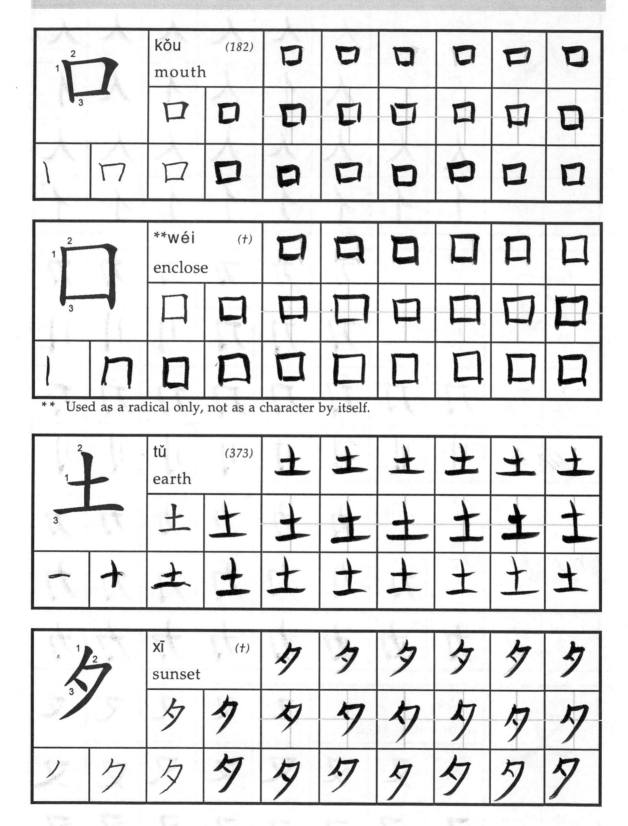

| kǒu (182) mouth | | | | | | | |

| **wéi (†) enclose | | | | | | | |

** Used as a radical only, not as a character by itself.

| tǔ (373) earth | | | | | | | |

| xī (†) sunset | | | | | | | |

大	dà (17) big; large	大	大	大	大	大	大
大	大	大	大	大	大	大	大
一	ナ	大	大	大	大	大	大	大	大

女	nǚ (299) female; woman	女	女	女	女	女	女
女	女	女	女	女	女	女	女
く	女	女	女	女	女	女	女	女	女

子	zǐ (24) son	子	子	子	子	子	子
子	子	子	子	子	子	子	子
了	了	子	子	子	子	子	子	子	子

寸	cùn (†) inch	寸	寸	寸	寸	寸	寸
寸	寸	寸	寸	寸	寸	寸	寸
一	寸	寸	寸	寸	寸	寸	寸	寸	寸

小	xiǎo (50) little; small	小	小	小	小	小	小
工	gōng (55) labor; work	工	工	工	工	工	工
幺	yāo (†) tiny; small	幺	幺	幺	幺	幺	幺
弓	gōng (†) bow	弓	弓	弓	弓	弓	弓

门	mén (199) door	门	门	门	门	门	门
	门 門	门	门	门	门	门	门
丶 丨 门 门	门	门	门	门	门	门

马	mǎ (359) horse	马	马	马	马	马	马
	马 馬						
乛 马 马						

心	xīn (82) heart	心	心	心	心	心	心
	心 忄						
丶 心 心 心						
丶 忄 忄						

戈	gē (†) dagger-axe	戈	戈	戈	戈	戈	戈
	戈						
一 弋 戈 戈						

	shǒu (115) hand	手	手	手	手	手	手
手	手 才						
一 二 三 手							
一 十 才							

	rì (269) sun	日	日	日	日	日	日
日	日						
丨 冂 日 日							

	yuè (207) moon	月	月	月	月	月	月
月	月						
丿 几 月 月							

	bèi (†) cowry shell	贝	贝	贝	贝	贝	贝
贝	贝 貝						
丨 冂 贝 贝							

火	huǒ (308) fire	火	火	火	火	火	火
	火 灬						
丶 丷 丷 火							
丿 八 灬 灬							

木	mù (607) wood	木	木	木	木	木	木
	木						
一 十 才 木							

水	shuǐ (102) water	水	水	水	水	水	水
	水 氵						
亅 扌 水 水							
丶 氵 氵							

田	tián (727) field	田	田	田	田	田	田
	田						
丨 冂 冂 田 田							

¹²³⁴⁵ 目	mù (408) eye	目	目	目	目	目	目
	目						
丨	冂	月	月	目			

¹²⁴³⁵ 示	shì (†) to show	示	示	示	示	示	示
	示　礻						
一	二	于	亓	示			
丶	冫	礻	礻				

¹²³⁵⁴⁶ 糸	**mì (†) fine silk	糸	糸	糸	糸	糸	糸
	纟　糸						
ㄑ	幺	幺	�End of	糸	糸		
ㄑ	幺	纟					

** Used as a radical only, not as a character by itself.

¹²⁴³⁵⁶ 耳	ěr (960) ear	耳	耳	耳	耳	耳	耳
	耳						
一	丁	下	下	耳	耳		

衣	yī (473) clothing	衣	衣	衣	衣	衣	衣
	衣 ／ 衤						
丶	亠	宀	𠂋	𧘇	衣		
丶	冫	衤	衤	衤			

言	yán (655) speech	言	言	言	言	言	言
	言 ／ 讠						
丶	亠	亠	言	言	言	言	
丶	讠						

走	zǒu (104) to walk	走	走	走	走	走	走
	走						
一	十	土	丰	丰	赱	走	

足	zú (758) foot	足	足	足	足	足	足
	足	卫					
丶	丨	口	口	무	무	足	
丶	丨	口	口	무	무	무	足

金	jīn (514) metal; gold	金	金	金	金	金	金
	金	钅					
丿	人	今	今	全	全	金	金
丿	𠂇	乇	钅	钅			

隹	zhuī (†) short-tailed bird	隹	隹	隹	隹	隹
	隹					
丿	亻	个	广	佇	佇	佳	隹

雨	yǔ (542) rain	雨	雨	雨	雨	雨	雨
	雨	雹						
一	一	一	一	冂	币	雨	雨	雨	
一	一	一	冂	币	雨	雨	雨	雹	

食	shí (549) to eat	食	食	食	食	食	食
	食	食						
丿	人	仐	今	今	今	食	食	食	
丿	人	仐	今	今	今	食	食		

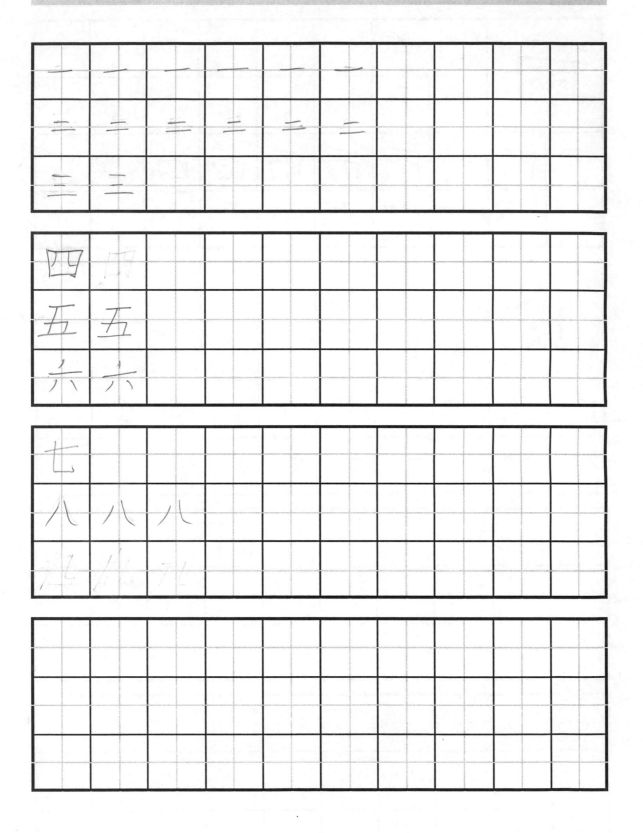

LESSONS

Dialogue I

先	xiān (179) first	先	先	先	先	先	先
	先	先	先	先	先	先	先	先
	ノ	丿	土	生	步	先	先	先	先	先

生	shēng (42) to be born	生	生	生	生	生	生
	生	生	生	生	生	生	生	生
	ノ	丿	仁	牛	生	生	生	生	生	生

你	nǐ (20) you	你	你	你	你	你	你
	你	你	你	你	你	你	你	你
	亻	亻	仁	你	你	你	你	你	你	你

好	hǎo (40) fine; good; OK	好	好	好	好	好
	好	好	好	好	好	好	好	好
	女	好	好	好	好	好	好	好	好

(19)

姐
姐

xiǎo (50) little; small	小	小	小	小	小	小
小	小	小	小	小	小	小	小
小	小	小	小	小	小	小	小	小

jiě (693) older sister	姐	姐	姐	姐	姐	姐
姐	姐	姐	姐	姐	姐	姐	姐
女	如	姐	姐	姐	姐	姐	姐	姐	姐

wáng (863) (a surname); king	王	王	王	王	王
王	王	王	王	王	王	王	王
一	二	干	王	王	王	王	王	王	王

lǐ (†) (a surname); plum	李	李	李	李	李
李	李	李	李	李	李	李	李
木	李	李	李	李	李	李	李	李	李

Dialogue II

是	shì (4) to be	是	是	是	是	是	是
	是	是	是	是	是	是	是	是
日	旦	早	早	�爿	是	是	是	是	是

老	lǎo (87) old	老	老	老	老	老	老
	老	老	老	老	老	老	老	老
一	十	土	耂	耂	老	老	老	老	老

师	shī (310) teacher	师	师	师	师	师	师	师
	师	師	师	师	师	师	师	师	师
l	リ	丿	师	师	师	师	师	师	师

吗	ma (248) QP	吗	吗	吗	吗	吗	吗	吗
	吗	嗎	吗	吗	吗	吗	吗	吗
口	吗	吗	吗	吗	吗	吗	吗	吗	吗

不	bù (5) not; no	不	不	不	不	不	不
不	不	不	不	不	不	不
一	丁	不	不	不	不	不	不	不	不

学	xué (46) to study	学	学	学	学	学	学
学	學	学	学	学	学	学	学
丶	丷	⺍	⺍	兴	学	学	学	学	学

也	yě (30) too; also	也	也	也	也	也	也
也	也	也	也	也	也	也	也
乛	九	也	也	也	也	也	也	也	也

中	zhōng (61) center; middle	中	中	中	中	中
中	中	中	中	中	中	中	中
丨	冂	口	中	中	中	中	中	中	中

国	guó (37) country	国	国	国	国	国	国
	国	國	国	国	国	国	国	国
丨	冂	冂	月	用	囯	囯	囯	囯	国
国	国	国	国	国	国	国	国	国	国

人	rén (9) person; people	人	人	人	人	人
	人							
人	人	人	人	人	人	人	人	人	人

美	měi (593) beautiful	美	美	美	美	美	美
	美	美	美	美	美	美	美	美
丶	丷	丷	兰	羊	羊	美	美	美	美

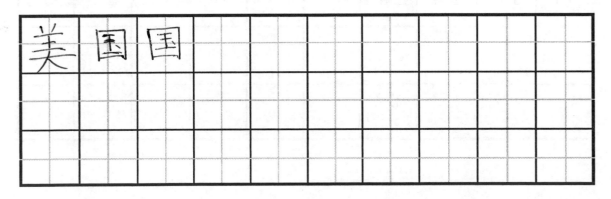

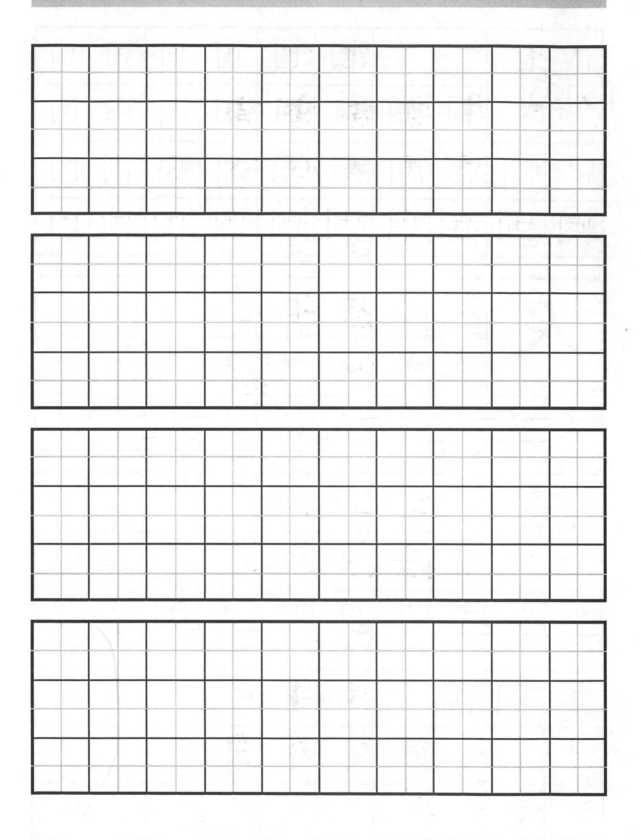

Dialogue I

呀	ya (267) P	呀	呀	呀	呀	呀	呀
	呀	呀	呀	呀	呀	呀	呀
口	口	吖	呀	呀	呀	呀	呀	呀

进	jìn (81) to enter	进	进	进	进	进	进
	进	進	进	进	进	进	进	进
一	二	井	井	丼	讲	进	进	进	进

快	kuài (223) fast; quick(ly)	快	快	快	快	快	快
	快	快	快	快	快	快	快	快
忄	忄	忆	快	快	快	快	快	快	快

来	lái (13) to come	来	来	来	来	来	来
	来	來	来	来	来	来	来	来
一	二	三	立	半	来	来	来	来	来
来	来	来	来	来	来	来	来	来	来

介	jiè (†) between	介	介	介	介	介	介
	介	介	介	介	介	介	介
人	个	介	介	介	介	介	介	介

绍	shào (†) carry on	绍	绍	绍	绍	绍	绍
	绍	紹	绍	绍	绍	绍	绍	绍
纟	纫	绍	绍	绍	绍	绍	绍	绍

下	xià (36) below; under	下	下	下	下	下	下
	下	下	下	下	下	下	下
一	丁	下	下	下	下	下	下	下

漂	piào (†) *pretty	漂	漂	漂	漂	漂	漂
	漂	漂	漂	漂	漂	漂	漂
氵	氵	氵	沂	沪	泗	湮	漂	漂
漂	漂	漂	漂	漂	漂	漂	漂	漂

Dialogue I

周	zhōu (690) week	周	周	周	周	周	周
	周 週	周	周	周	周	周	周
ノ	几	月	用	用	用	周	周	周	周
周	周	周	周	周	周	周	周	周	周

末	mò (†) end	末	末	末	末	末	末
	末	末	末	末	末	末	末
一	二	千	才	末	末	末	末	末	末

打	dǎ (136) to hit; to strike	打	打	打	打	打
	打	打	打	打	打	打	打	打
才	打	打	打	打	打	打	打	打

球	qiú (605) ball	球	球	球	球	球	球
	球	球	球	球	球	球	球	球
王	王一	玎	玙	玙	球	球	球	球	球

看	kàn (41) to watch; to look	看	看	看	看	看
	看	看	看	看	看	看	看	看
	一	二	三	手	看	看	看	看	看	看

(Please note that the first stroke goes down from right to left.)

电	diàn (77) electric	电	电	电	电	电	电
	电	電	电	电	电	电	电	电
	丨	冂	曰	日	电	电	电	电	电	电

视	shì (612) vision	视	视	视	视	视	视
	视	視	视	视	视	视	视	视
	礻	视	视	视	视	视	视	视	视

唱	chàng (679) to sing	唱	唱	唱	唱	唱	唱
	唱	唱	唱	唱	唱	唱	唱	唱
	口	口日	唱	唱	唱	唱	唱	唱	唱

PAT REQUA

歌	gē (725) song	歌	歌	歌	歌	歌	歌
	歌	歌	歌	歌	歌	歌	歌	歌
哥	歌	歌	歌	歌	歌	歌	歌	歌

跳	tiào (611) to jump	跳	跳	跳	跳	跳	跳
	跳	跳	跳	跳	跳	跳	跳	跳
足	趴	趴	趴	跳	跳	跳	跳	跳	跳
跳	跳	跳	跳	跳	跳	跳	跳	跳	跳

舞	wǔ (954) to dance; dance	舞	舞	舞	舞	舞
	舞	舞	舞	舞	舞	舞	舞	舞
ノ	㇒	𠂉	午	缶	舞	無	無	舞	舞
舞	舞	舞	舞	舞	舞	舞	舞	舞	舞

✓

听	tīng (161) to listen	听	听	听	听	听	听
	听 聽	听	听	听	听	听	听
口	叮	叮	听	听	听	听	听	听

音	yīn (487) sound	音	音	音	音	音	音
	音	音	音	音	音	音	音
丶	亠	立	立	立	音	音	音	音	音

乐	yuè (713) music	乐	乐	乐	乐	乐	乐
	乐 樂	乐	乐	乐	乐	乐	乐
一	匚	乐	乐	乐	乐	乐	乐	乐

对	duì (60) correct; right; toward	对	对	对	对	对
	对 對	对	对	对	对	对	对
又	对	对	对	对	对	对	对	对

PAT REQUA

		shí (34) time	时	时	时	时	时	时
时		时	時	时	时	时	时	时	时
日	时	时	时	时	时	时	时	时

		hòu (147) to wait	候	候	候	候	候	候
候		候	候	候	候	候	候	候	候
亻	亻	仁	仁	侯	侯	侯	候	候	候

		shū (238) book	书	书	书	书	书	书
书		书	書	书	书	书	书	书	书
乛	乛	书	书	书	书	书	书	书	书

		yǐng (399) shadow	影	影	影	影	影	影
影		影	影	影	影	影	影	影	影
日	日	旦	暑	景	景	景	景	景	景
影	影	影	影	影	影	影	影	影	影

常	cháng (202) often	常	常	常	常	常	常	常
	常	常	常	常	常	常	常	常
丶	丷	屵	屵	屵	峃	峃	峃	常
常	常	常	常	常	常	常	常	常	常

去	qù (29) to go	去	去	去	去	去	去
	去	去	去	去	去	去	去	去
一	十	土	去	去	去	去	去	去	去

外	wài (141) outside	外	外	外	外	外	外
	外	外	外	外	外	外	外	外
夕	夘	外	外	外	外	外	外	外	外

客	kè (532) guest	客	客	客	客	客	客
	客	客	客	客	客	客	客	客
宀	宀	宀	安	客	客	客	客	客	客

昨	zuó　　　(†) yesterday	昨	昨	昨	昨	昨	昨
昨	昨	昨	昨	昨	昨	昨	昨
日	昨	昨	昨	昨	昨	昨	昨	昨

所	suǒ　　　(127) *so; place	所	所	所	所	所	所
所	所	所	所	所	所	所	所
⼂	⼍	戶	戶	戶	所	所	所	所	所

以	yǐ　　　(44) with	以	以	以	以	以	以
以	以	以	以	以	以	以	以
⼂	⼂	以	以	以	以	以	以	以

亮	liàng (538) bright	亮	亮	亮	亮	亮	亮
	亮	亮	亮	亮	亮	亮	亮
亠	古	产	亨	亭	亮	亮	亮	亮	亮

坐	zuò (371) to sit	坐	坐	坐	坐	坐	坐
	坐	坐	坐	坐	坐	坐	坐
人	从	丛	坐	坐	坐	坐	坐	坐	坐

哪	nǎ / něi (275) QW; which	哪	哪	哪	哪	哪	哪
	哪	哪	哪	哪	哪	哪	哪
口	叮	吗	叨	明	明3	哪	哪	哪	哪

工	gōng (55) craft	工	工	工	工	工	工
	工	工	工	工	工	工	工
一	丁	工	工	工	工	工	工	工	工

作	zuò (214) to work; to do	作	作	作	作	作
	作	作	作	作	作	作	作
亻 作		作	作	作	作	作	作	作

校	xiào (636) school	校	校	校	校	校	校
	校	校	校	校	校	校	校	校
木	木	术	栌	栌	栌	校	校	校	校	校

喝	hē (720) to drink	喝	喝	喝	喝	喝	喝
	喝						
口	叩	叩	吗	喝	喝		

茶	chá (985) tea	茶	茶	茶	茶	茶	茶
	茶	茶					
一	十	艹	艾	苂	芧	茅	茶	

咖	kā (†) *coffee	咖	咖	咖	咖	咖	咖
	咖						
口 叻 咖							

啡	fēi (†) *coffee	啡	啡	啡	啡	啡	啡
	啡						
口 叮 叮 哔 哗 唯 啡 啡 啡							

啤	pí (†) *beer	啤	啤	啤	啤	啤	啤
	啤						
口 口 叫 叭 咱 咱 啤 嘤 啤							

酒	jiǔ (858) wine	酒	酒	酒	酒	酒	酒
	酒						
氵 氵 汀 沔 洒 洒 酒							

吧	ba (175) P	吧	吧	吧	吧	吧	吧
	吧						
口	吧						

要	yào (25) to want	要	要	要	要	要	要
	要						
一	一	一	西	西	西	要	

杯	bēi (†) cup; glass	杯	杯	杯	杯	杯	杯
	杯						
木	杯						

起	qǐ (47) to rise	起	起	起	起	起	起
	起						
十	土	丰	丰	走	走	起	起	起

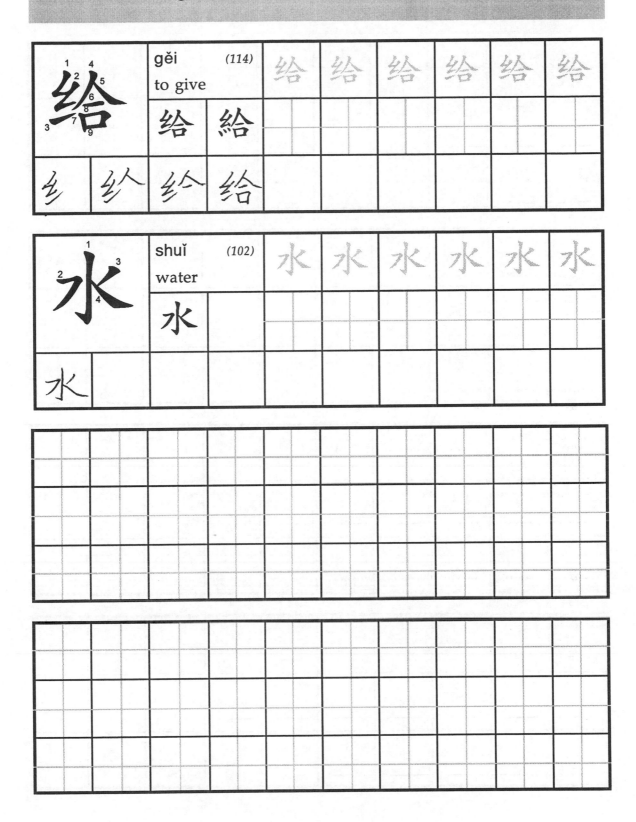

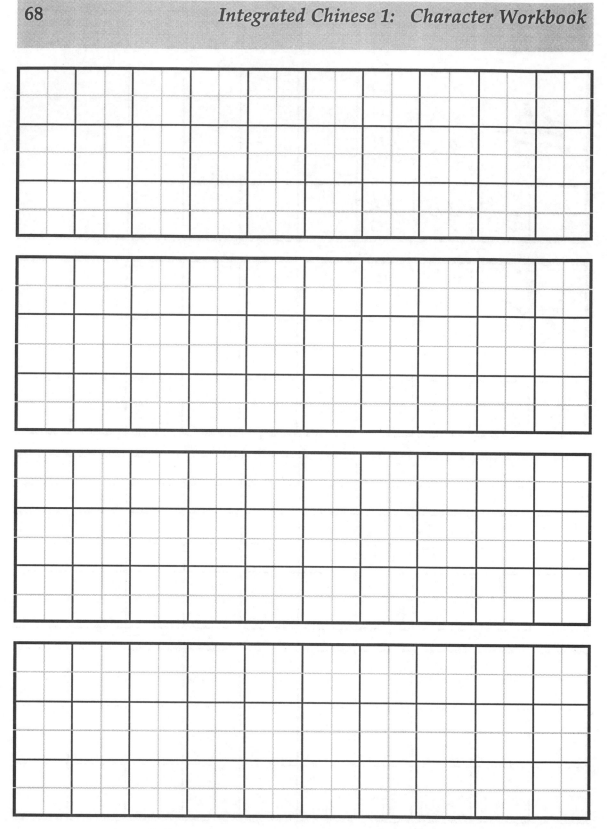

Dialogue II

	wán (970) to have a visit; to play	玩	玩	玩	玩	玩
玩	玩					
王	珒	玩				

	tú (7) drawing	图	图	图	图	图	图
图	图	圖					
冂	冂	冈	図	冬	图	图	

	guǎn (938) accomodations	馆	馆	馆	馆	馆
馆	馆	館				
乍	饣	饣	馆	馆	馆	馆

	píng (†) bottle	瓶	瓶	瓶	瓶	瓶	瓶
瓶	瓶						
丶	丷	丷	兰	芓	并	并	瓶	瓶	瓶

	liáo (忄) to chat	聊	聊	聊	聊	聊	聊
	聊						
耳	耴	耴	耴	聊	聊		

	cái (162) not until	才	才	才	才	才	才
	才						
一	十	才					

	huí (108) to return	回	回	回	回	回	回
	回						
丨	冂	回	回				

Dialogue I

		huà (137) speech	话	话	话	话	话	话
话		话 話						
	丶	讠	讠	讠	讠	讠	话	话

		wèi (†) Hello!; Hey!	喂	喂	喂	喂	喂	喂
喂		喂						
	口	吧	吧	喂	喂	喂		

		jiù (19) then	就	就	就	就	就	就
就		就						
	亠	古	京	京	就	就	就	

		wèi (†) M (polite)	位	位	位	位	位	位
位		位						
	亻	亻	位	位	位	位		

午	wǔ (882) noon	午	午	午	午	午	午
	午						
ノ	⺄	二	午				

间	jiān (156) M (for rooms)	间	间	间	间	间	
	间	間					
门	间						

题	tí (224) topic; question	题	题	题	题	题	
	题	題					
日	旦	早	早	昰	是	是	是	题

开	kāi (94) to open; to hold	开	开	开	开	开	
	开	開					
一	二	于	开				

会	huì (32) to meet		会	会	会	会	会	会
	会	會						
人	人	仝	会	会				

节	jié (555) M (for classes)		节	节	节	节	节	
	节	節						
艹	节	节						

课	kè (762) class; lesson		课	课	课	课	课	课
	课	課						
讠	订	叮	诩	诩	诅	评	课	课

级	jí (172) level; rank		级	级	级	级	级	级
	级	級						
纟	纠	级	级					

考	kǎo (767) to give or take a test	考	考	考	考	考
	考					
一	十	土	耂	耂	考	

试	shì (701) to try; to test	试	试	试	试	试	试
	试	試					
讠	讠	订	订	讠	试	试	

后	hòu (73) after; rear	后	后	后	后	后	后
	后	後					
丿	厂	斤	后				

空	kòng (340) free time	空	空	空	空	空	空
	空						
宀	宀	穴	空				

方	fāng (96) square	方	方	方	方	方	方
	方						
丶	亠	方	方				

便	biàn / pián (282) convenient / *cheap	便	便	便	便	便	
	便						
亻	仁	佰	俥	便			

到	dào (22) to go to; to arrive	到	到	到	到	到	
	到						
一	乙	云	至	到			

办	bàn (313) to manage	办	办	办	办	办	办
	办	辦					
フ	力	力	办				

		gōng (259) public	公	公	公	公	公	公
公	公							
八	公	公						

		shì (669) room	室	室	室	室	室	室
室	室							
宀	宀	宓	宊	宊	室	室		

		xíng (99) be all right; OK	行	行	行	行	行	
行	行							
彳	彳	行	行					

		děng (35) to wait	等	等	等	等	等	等
等	等							
竹	竺	等						

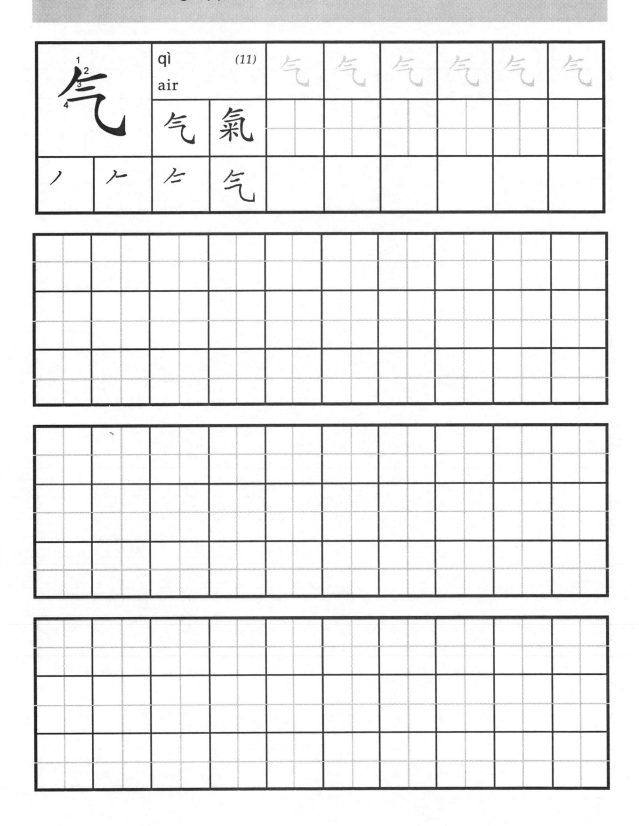

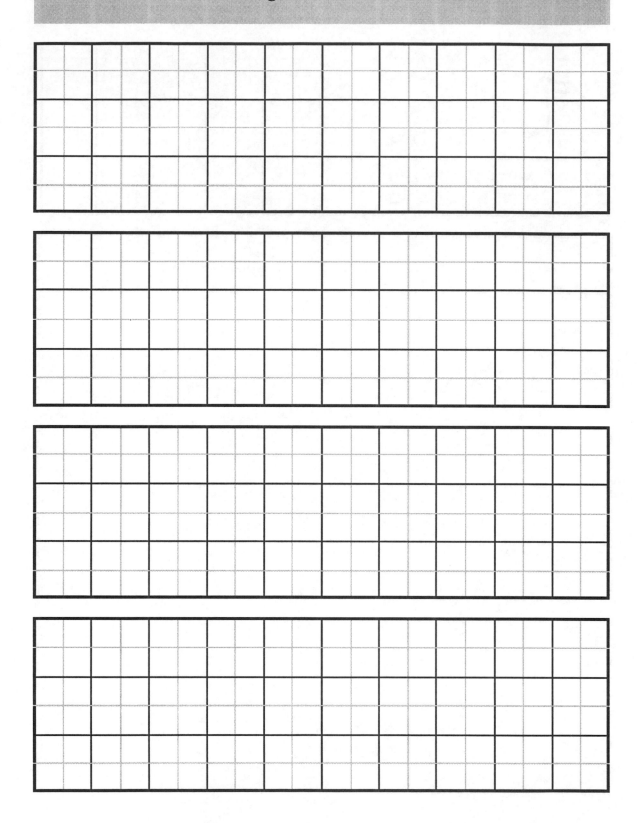

Dialogue II

	bāng (536) to help	帮	帮	帮	帮	帮	帮
帮	帮 幫						
一 二	三	丰	丰3	邦	邦	帮	帮

	gēn (247) with; to follow	跟	跟	跟	跟	跟	
跟	跟						
足 跟							

	liàn (950) to drill	练	练	练	练	练	练
练	练 練						
纟 纟 纟 练	练 练						

	xí (417) to practice	习	习	习	习	习	习
习	习 習						
丁 习 习							

说	shuō (21) to speak	说	说	说	说	说	说
	说	説					
讠	讠	讠	讠	讠	说	说	说

啊	a (254) P	啊	啊	啊	啊	啊	啊
	啊						
口	叮	叮	吖	啊	啊		

但	dàn (150) but	但	但	但	但	但	但
	但						
亻	佢	但					

知	zhī (131) to know	知	知	知	知	知	知
	知						
丿	卜	纟	午	矢	知		

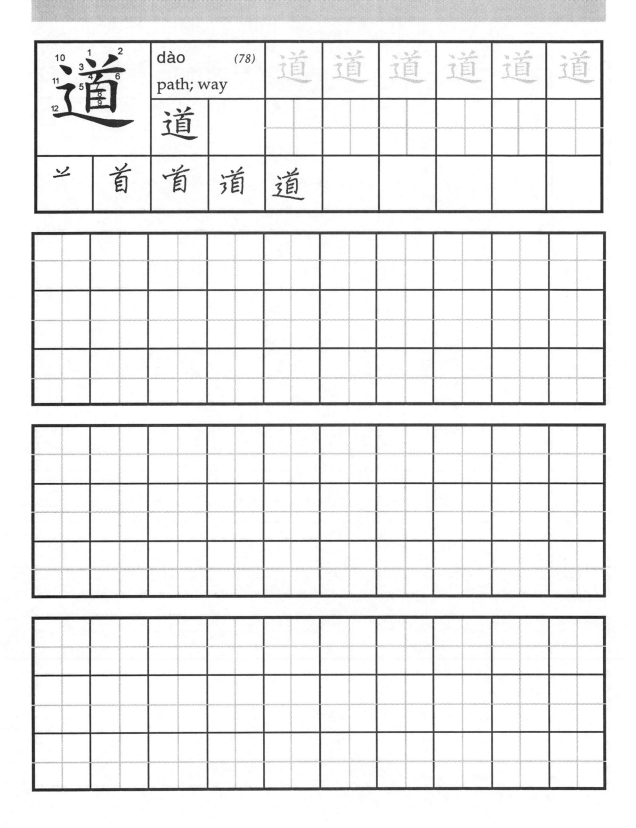

道	dào (78) path; way	道	道	道	道	道	道
	道						
丷	首	首	道	道			

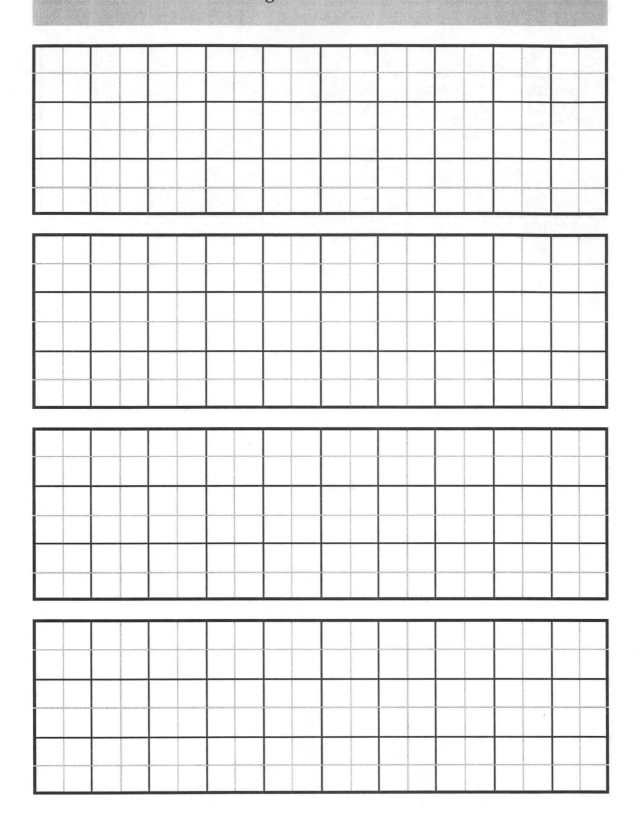

Dialogue I

	zhù (632) to assist	助	助	助	助	助	助
助	助						
且	助						

	fù (525) duplicate	复	复	复	复	复	复
复	复 復						
ノ	亻	旨	尸	复	复		

	xiě (317) to write	写	写	写	写	写	写
写	写 寫						
ノ	冖	宀	写	写			

	màn (657) slow	慢	慢	慢	慢	慢	慢
慢	慢						
忄	忄曰	惺	慢				

教	jiāo (244) to teach	教	教	教	教	教	教
	教 教△						
十	土	尹	孝	孝	教	教	

笔	bǐ (775) pen	笔	笔	笔	笔	笔	笔
	笔 筆						
灶	丛	竺	竺	笔			

难	nán (285) difficult	难	难	难	难	难	难
	难 難						
又	刈	难					

里	lǐ (26) inside	里	里	里	里	里	里
	里 裡 裏						
日	甲	甲	里				

第　dì　(211)　(ordinal prefix)

第　第　第　第　第　第

第

⺮　第

预　yù　(892)　to prepare

预　预　预　预　预　预

预　预

一　マ　孑　予　预

语　yǔ　(706)　language

语　语　语　语　语　语

语　語

讠　讠　订　诬　语　语

法　fǎ　(142)　method; way

法　法　法　法　法　法

法

氵　法

容	róng (421) hold; contain; allow	容	容	容	容	容
	容					
宀	宀	宊	容				

易	yì (582) easy	易	易	易	易	易	易
	易					
日	月	马	易	易			

懂	dǒng (269) to understand	懂	懂	懂	懂	懂
	懂	懂				
忄	忄	忄	忄	愔	懂	懂	懂

词	cí (†) word	词	词	词	词	词	词
	词	詞				
讠	讠	讠	词				

汉	hàn (t) Chinese	汉	汉	汉	汉	汉	汉
	汉 漢						
氵 汉							

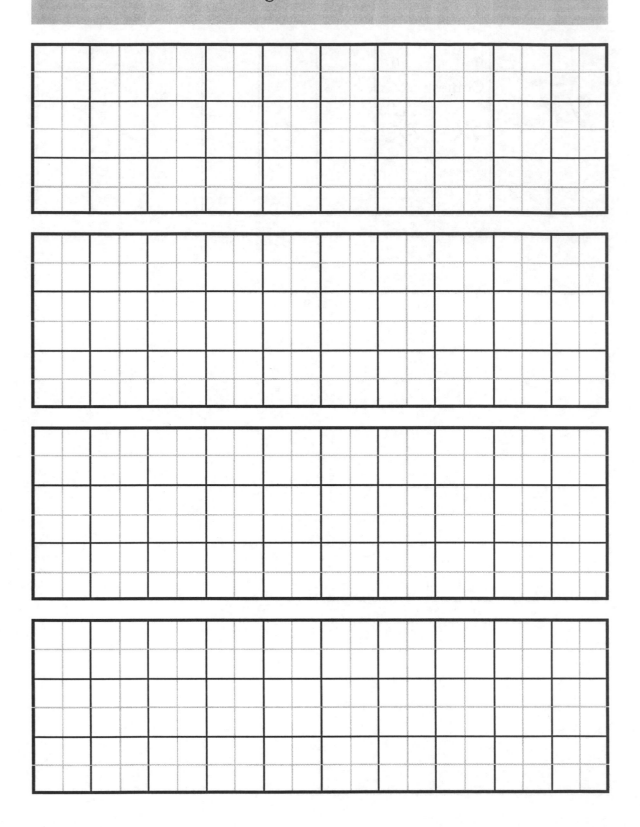

Dialogue II

平	píng (232) level; even	平	平	平	平	平	平
	平						
一	丆	刁	亚	平			

早	zǎo (344) early	早	早	早	早	早	早
	早						
日	旦	早					

夜	yè (405) night	夜	夜	夜	夜	夜	夜
	夜						
一	亠	疒	疒	夜	夜		

功	gōng (681) skill	功	功	功	功	功	功
	功						
工	功						

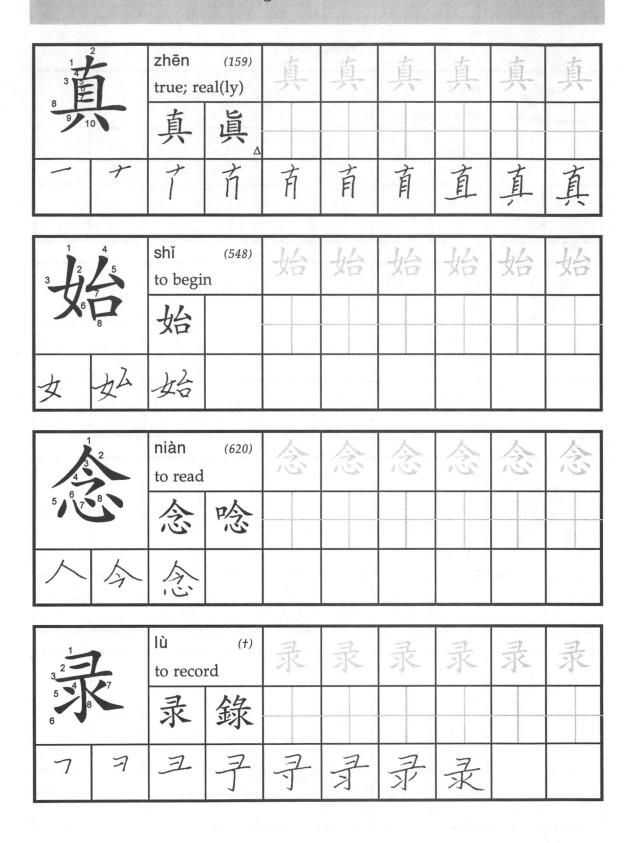

帅	shuài (t) handsome; smart	帅	帅	帅	帅	帅
	帅　帥					
ノ	リ	帅				

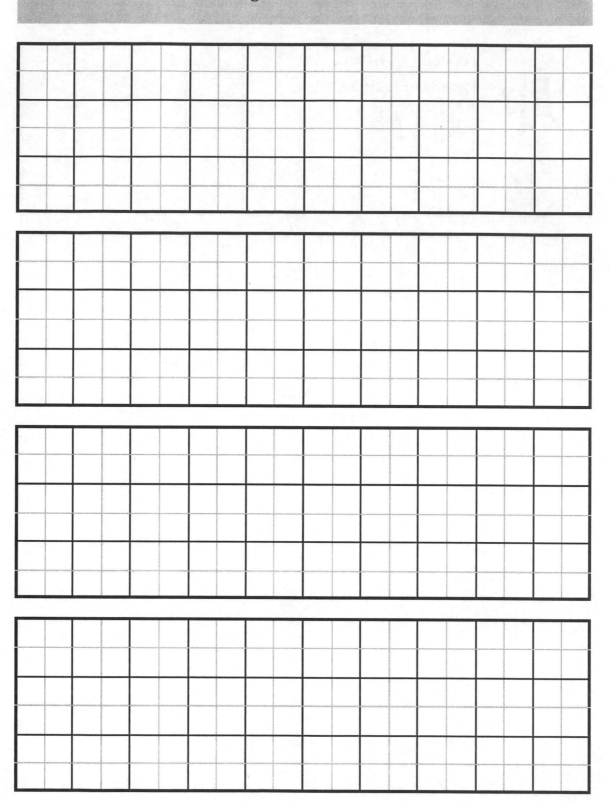

Dialogue I

篇	piān (†) M (for articles)	篇	篇	篇	篇	篇
	篇					
烒	烒	竻	竻	笓	笒	笁	篤	篇	篇

记	jì (289) record	记	记	记	记	记	记
	记	記					
讠	订	记	记				

床	chuáng (682) bed	床	床	床	床	床	床
	床	牀					
丶	亠	广	床				

洗	xǐ (860) to wash	洗	洗	洗	洗	洗	洗
	洗						
氵	汫	沪	浐	浐	洗	洗

| 澡 | zǎo (忄) bath 澡 | | 澡 | 澡 | 澡 | 澡 | 澡 | 澡 |
| シ | シア | シア | 澡 | 澡 | | | | | |

| 边 | biān (140) side 边 邊 | | 边 | 边 | 边 | 边 | 边 | 边 |
| 力 | 力 | 边 | | | | | | | |

| 发 | fā (64) to emit; to issue 发 發 | | 发 | 发 | 发 | 发 | 发 | |
| ㇄ | 屮 | 岁 | 发 | 发 | | | | | |

| 脑 | nǎo (600) brain 脑 腦 | | 脑 | 脑 | 脑 | 脑 | 脑 | 脑 |
| 月 | 月 | 肜 | 肔 | 胶 | 脑 | 脑 | | | |

餐	cān meal	(†)	餐	餐	餐	餐	餐	餐
	餐							
丶	丷	夕	夗	夗	癸	癸	癸	餐
餐	餐	餐						

厅	tīng hall	(†)	厅	厅	厅	厅	厅	厅
	厅	廳						
一	厂	厅	厅					

报	bào newspaper	(333)	报	报	报	报	报	报
	报	報						
扌	扫	扫	报					

宿	sù to stay	(†)	宿	宿	宿	宿	宿	宿
	宿							
宀	宁	宿	宿					

舍	shè *(†)* house	舍	舍	舍	舍	舍	舍	舍
	舍							
人	스	今	全	舍				

正	zhèng *(†)* just	正	正	正	正	正	正	正
	正							
一	丁	丅	疋	正				

前	qián *(91)* front; before	前	前	前	前	前	前	前
	前							
丶	丷	丷	首	前				

告	gào *(346)* to tell; to inform	告	告	告	告	告		
	告							
丿	丷	屮	屮	告				

诉	sù (545) to tell; to relate	诉	诉	诉	诉	诉
	诉 訴					
讠 诉 诉						

已	yǐ (171) already	已	已	已	已	已
	已					
フ コ 已						

经	jīng (76) pass through	经	经	经	经	经
	经 經					
纟 纟 纟 经						

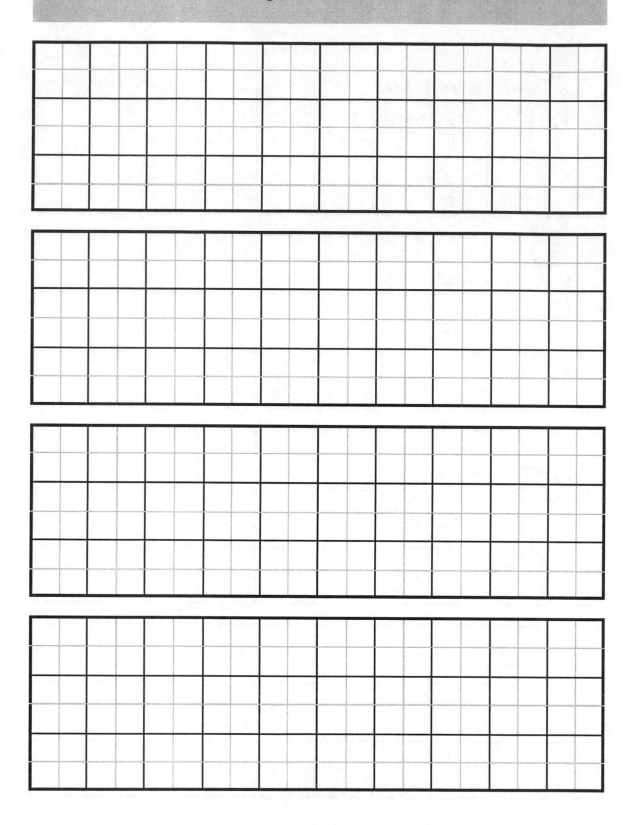

Dialogue II

封	fēng (689)	封	封	封	封	封	封
	M (for letters)						
	封						
土 圭 封	封						

信	xìn (318)	信	信	信	信	信	信
	letter						
	信						
亻 信							

最	zuì (174)	最	最	最	最	最	
	(superalative); most						
	最						
日 胃 最	最						

近	jìn (414)	近	近	近	近	近	近
	near						
	近						
斤 近							

除	chú (562) except	除	除	除	除	除	除
	除						
阝	阝	队	阝	除	除	除	

专	zhuān (519) special	专	专	专	专	专	专
	专 專						
一	二	专	专				

业	yè (†) occupation; profession	业	业	业	业	业	
	业 業						
丨	丬	业	业	业			

惯	guàn (†) to be used to	惯	惯	惯	惯	惯	惯
	惯 惯						
忄	忄	忄	忄	惯	惯		

清	qīng (381) clear; clean	清	清	清	清	清	清
	清						
氵	清						

楚	chǔ (907) clear; neat	楚	楚	楚	楚	楚	楚
	楚						
木	林	替	梺	梺	梺	楚	

步	bù (314) step	步	步	步	步	步	步
	步						
丨	卜	止	止	丗	丗	步	

希	xī (818) hope	希	希	希	希	希	希
	希						
丿	乂	㐅	爻	希			

望	wàng (298) hope; expect	望	望	望	望	望	望
	望 望						
、	二	亠	亡	切	切	切	切	望	望
望							

能	néng (52) to be able	能	能	能	能	能	能
	能						
ㄙ	ㄙ	育	育	能	能	能	

用	yòng (59) to use	用	用	用	用	用	用
	用						
ノ	几	月	月	用			

笑	xiào (250) to laugh	笑	笑	笑	笑	笑	笑
	笑						
灶	灶	竺	竿	笑			

祝	zhù (†) to wish	祝	祝	祝	祝	祝	祝
	祝						
丶	亠	礻	礻	初	初	祝	

Dialogue I

	mǎi (460) to buy		买	买	买	买	买	买
买	买	買						
一	乛	乛	三	买	买			

	dōng (234) east		东	东	东	东	东	东
东	东	東						
一	七	专	夯	东				

	xī (225) west		西	西	西	西	西	西
西	西							
一	一	一	丙	西	西			

	shòu (†) to sell		售	售	售	售	售	售
售	售							
隹	售							

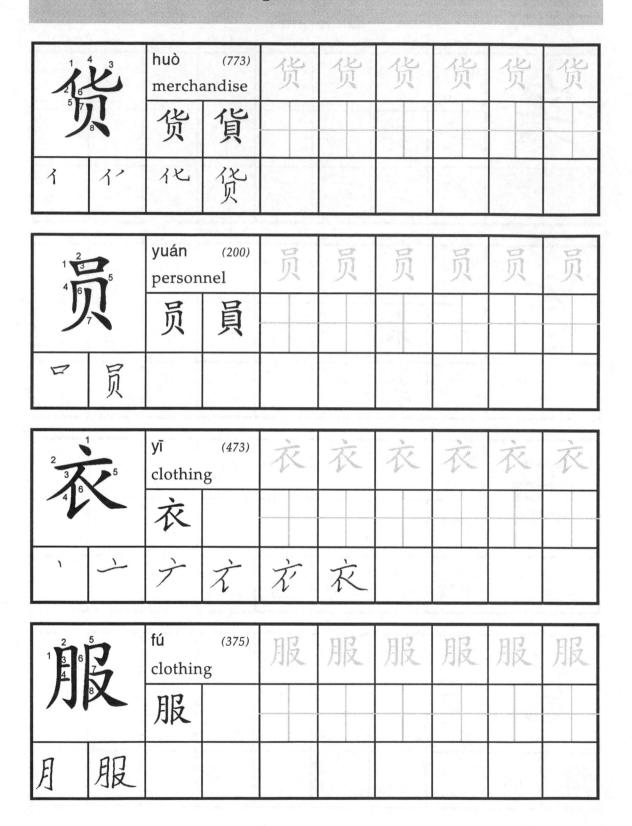

件	jiàn (311) M (for items)	件		件	件	件	件	件	件
	件								
亻	亻	仁	仁	件					

衬	chèn (†) lining	衬		衬	衬	衬	衬	衬	衬
	衬	襯							
衤	衤	衬	衬						

衫	shān (†) shirt	衫		衫	衫	衫	衫	衫	衫
	衫								
丶	冫	衤	衤	衤	衤	衫	衫		

颜	yán (†) face; countenance	颜		颜	颜	颜	颜	颜
	颜	顏						
丶	亠	六	立	立	产	彦	颜	

色	sè (287) color	色	色	色	色	色	色	色
	色							
ノ	ク	色						

黄	huáng (638) yellow	黄	黄	黄	黄	黄	黄	黄
	黄	黄						
一	十	サ	世	芹	苦	苗	苗	黄
黄								

红	hóng (352) red	红	红	红	红	红	红
	红	红					
纟	红						

穿	chuān (539) to wear	穿	穿	穿	穿	穿	穿
	穿						
宀	空	空	穿	穿			

条	tiáo (213) M (for long objects)		条	条	条	条	条
	条	條					
ノ	ク	夂	冬	夅	夅	条	

裤	kù (†) pants		裤	裤	裤	裤	裤	裤
	裤	裤					
衤	衤	衤	裤	裤	裤		

宜	yí (†) suitable; *cheap		宜	宜	宜	宜	宜
	宜						
宀	宜						

付	fù (†) to pay		付	付	付	付	付	付
	付						
亻	付						

钱	qián (398) money	钱	钱	钱	钱	钱	钱
	钱	錢						
𡿨	𡿨	𡿨	钅	钱	钱			

共	gòng (283) altogether	共	共	共	共	共	共
	共							
一	十	卄	共	共	共			

少	shǎo (192) few	少	少	少	少	少	少
	少							
小	少							

块	kuài (403) piece; dollar	块	块	块	块	块	块
	块	塊						
一	十	土	块					

毛	máo (531) hair; dime	毛	毛	毛	毛	毛	毛
	毛						
ノ	二	三	毛				

分	fēn (90) penny; minute	分	分	分	分	分	
	分						
八	分						

百	bǎi (233) hundred	百	百	百	百	百	百
	百						
一	丆	百					

Dialogue II

		shuāng (729) M; pair	双	双	双	双	双	双
双		双 雙						
又	双							

		xié (901) shoe	鞋	鞋	鞋	鞋	鞋	鞋
鞋		鞋						
廿	甘	苷	革	軭	鞋			

		huàn (745) to (ex)change	换	换	换	换	换	换
换		换 换						
扌	扩	扩	护	护	拘	换	换	

黑	hēi (438) black	黑	黑	黑	黑	黑	黑
	黑						
丶	冂	冚	四	四	甲	甲	里	黑

虽	suí (603) though; while	虽	虽	虽	虽	虽
	虽 雖					
口	吕	吊	虽	虽			

然	rán (84) like that; so	然	然	然	然	然	然
	然						
夕	夕犬	夕犬	然				

合	hé (215) to suit; to agree	合	合	合	合	合
	合					
人	合	合				

	shì (757)	适	适	适	适	适	适
适	to suit; to fit						
	适 适						
丿 一 千 舌 适							

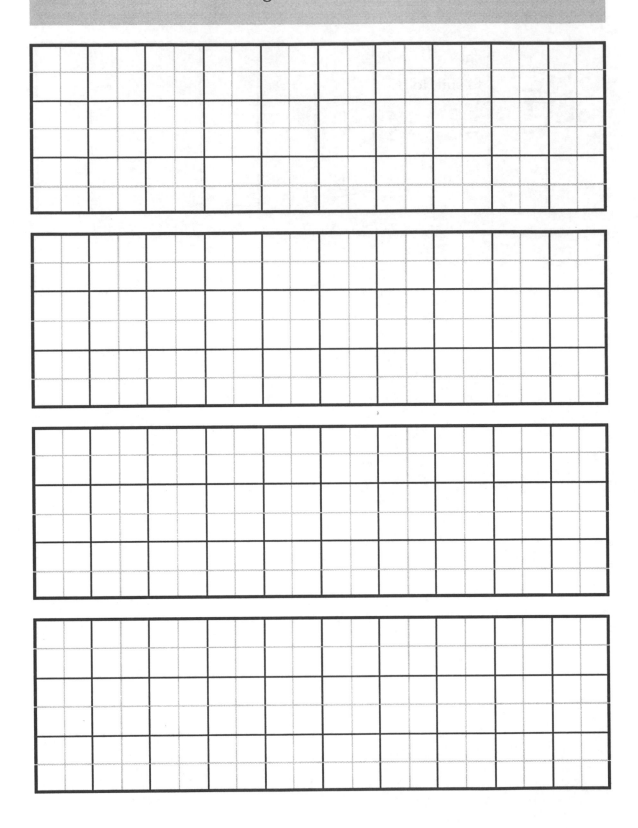

Dialogue I

	bǐ (206) to compare	比	比	比	比	比	比
比	比						
一 ヒ ヒ´ 比							

	yǔ (542) rain	雨	雨	雨	雨	雨	雨
雨	雨						
一 厂 丙 雨 雨 雨 雨 雨							

	gèng (260) even more	更	更	更	更	更	更
更	更						
一 百 更 更							

	ér (95) and; in addition	而	而	而	而	而	
而	而						
一 ア 广 丙 而 而							

且	qiě (355) for the time being	且	且	且	且	且
且					
丨	冂	冂	月	且		

暖	nuǎn (†) warm	暖	暖	暖	暖	暖	暖
暖						
日	日	日	日	日	日	日	日	暖

约	yuē (568) to make an appointment		约	约	约	约
约	約				
纟	纟	约	约		

园	yuán (898) garden	园	园	园	园	园	园
园	園					
丨	冂	冂	日	园	园	园

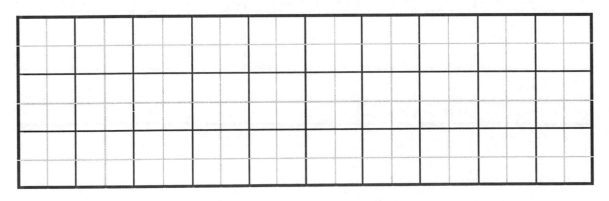

叶	yè (777)	叶	叶	叶	叶	叶	叶
	leaf						
	叶 葉						
口 口一 叶							

像	xiàng (†)	像	像	像	像	像	
	image; picture						
	像						
亻 亻 亻 侉 侉 侉 侉 俏 像							
像 像							

海	hǎi (348)	海	海	海	海	海	海
	sea						
	海						
氵 氵 汐 海 海 海 海							

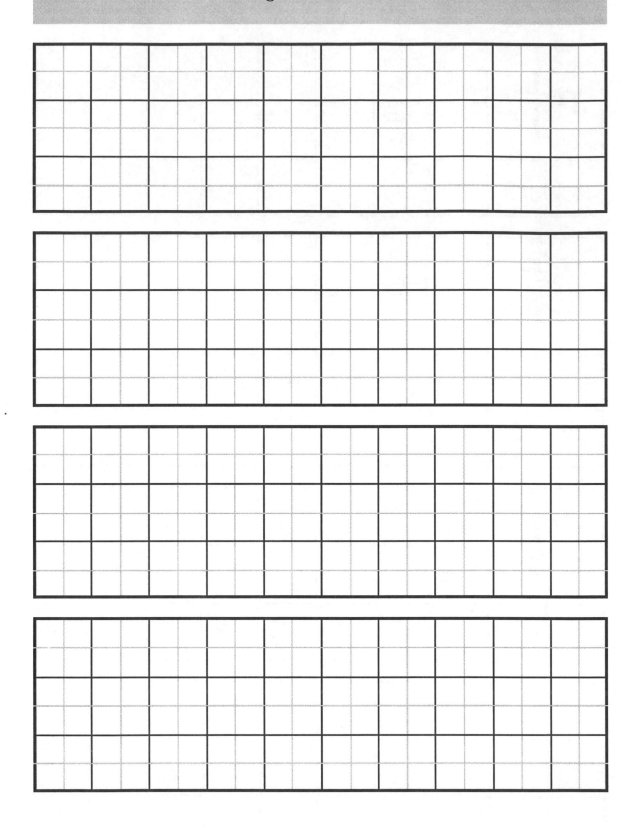

Dialogue II

糟	zāo (†) messy; in a mess	糟	糟	糟	糟	糟
	糟					
、	゛	⺌	屮	米	米	米	米	米	米
米	米	米	糟			

糕	gāo (†) cake	糕	糕	糕	糕	糕	糕
	糕						
米	米	糕					

又	yòu (65) again	又	又	又	又	又	又
	又						
乛	又						

刚	gāng (415) just now	刚	刚	刚	刚	刚	刚
	刚	剛					
丨	冂	刀	冈	冈刂	刚		

出	chū (35) to go out	出	出	出	出	出	出
	出						
凵	屮	屮	出	出			

热	rè (319) hot	热	热	热	热	热	热
	热	熱					
扌	扌	执	执	热			

舒	shū (†) stretch	舒	舒	舒	舒	舒	舒
	舒						
人	人	今	全	舍	舍丶	舍乛	舍彐	舒

夏	xià (†) summer	夏	夏	夏	夏	夏	夏
	夏						
一	𠂇	百	百	夏			

凉	liáng (†) cool	凉	凉	凉	凉	凉	凉
	凉	凉					
丶	冫	冫	广	泸	凉		

春	chūn (736) spring	春	春	春	春	春	春
	春						
一	二	三	丰	夫	春		

冬	dōng (†) winter	冬	冬	冬	冬	冬	冬
	冬						
丿	夂	冬	冬	冬			

	tái (526) platform; stage		台	台	台	台	台
台	台	臺 T					
	ㄥ	ㄙ	台				

	běi (464) north		北	北	北	北	北	北
北	北						
	丨	ㄦ	土	北			

	wān (†) strait; bay		湾	湾	湾	湾	湾	湾
湾	湾	灣					
	氵	氵	汋	汋	沖	沖	沐	湾

Dialogue I

寒	hán (†) winter	寒	寒	寒	寒	寒	寒
	寒						
宀	宀	宀	宀	宀	宀	宀	寒	寒

假	jià (831) vacation	假	假	假	假	假	假
	假						
亻	亻	亻	仴	仴	仴	仴	仴	假

飞	fēi (357) to fly	飞	飞	飞	飞	飞	飞
	飞	飛					
㇟	飞	飞					

机	jī (125) machine	机	机	机	机	机	机
	机	機					
木	朾	机					

票	piào (†) ticket	票	票	票	票	票	票
	票						
西	票						

场	chǎng (364) field	场	场	场	场	场	场
	场	場					
土	圬	场					

汽	qì (507) steam; gas	汽	汽	汽	汽	汽	汽
	汽						
氵	氵	汈	浐	汽			

车	chē (178) car; vehicle	车	车	车	车	车	车
	车	車					
一	士	车	车				

或	huò (331) or	或	或	或	或	或	或	或
或								
一	弋	豆	式	或	或			

者	zhě (258) P	者	者	者	者	者	者	者
者								
土	尹	者						

地	dì (16) ground	地	地	地	地	地	地	地
地								
士	地							

铁	tiě (439) iron	铁	铁	铁	铁	铁	铁	铁
铁	鐵							
金	钅	钅	铱	铗	铁			

走	zǒu (104) to walk	走	走	走	走	走	走
	走						
土	土	丰	卡	走	走			

站	zhàn (338) to stand; station	站	站	站	站	站	
	站						
丶	亠	亠	立	立	立	立	站	

绿	lǜ (851) green	绿	绿	绿	绿	绿	绿
	绿	綠					
纟	纟	纟	纟	纾	纾	纾	绿	绿

线	xiàn (263) line; route	线	线	线	线	线	线
	线	線					
纟	纟	纟	纹	线	线			

藍	lán blue (†)	藍	藍	藍	藍	藍	藍
	藍	藍					
艹	艹	芐	莎	莎	莜	莜	莒	蓝	藍

麻	má hemp (†)	麻	麻	麻	麻	麻	麻
	麻						
广	床	麻					

烦	fán to trouble (†)	烦	烦	烦	烦	烦	烦
	烦	煩					
丶	丷	火	火	烦			

租	zū to rent (†)	租	租	租	租	租	租
	租						
禾	租						

	sòng (469) to deliver; to see off; to send			送	送	送	送
送							
、	゛	丷	关	关	关	送	

Dialogue II

	guò (38) to pass	过	过	过	过	过	过
过	过　過						
	一　丁　寸　过						

	ràng (379) to let; to allow	让	让	让	让	让	
让	让　讓						
	讠　让						

	huā (240) flower; to spend	花	花	花	花	花	
花	花　花						
	艹　艻　花						

	měi (306) every; each	每	每	每	每	每	每
每	每						
	ノ　每						

速	sù (503) speed	速	速	速	速	速	速
	速						
一	戸	束	束	束	速		

路	lù (165) road; way	路	路	路	路	路	路
	路						
吊	趵	趵	趵	路			

緊	jǐn (412) tense; tight	緊	緊	緊	緊	緊	緊
	緊	緊					
刂	収	竪	緊				

自	zì (63) self; from	自	自	自	自	自	自
	自						
丿	自						

己	jǐ (130) self	己 己 己 己 己 己
己	
ㄱ ㄱ 己	

| 新 | xīn (181) new | 新 新 新 新 新 新 |
| 新 | |

礼	lǐ (†) ceremony	礼 礼 礼 礼 礼 礼
礼 禮	
ㄗ 礼	

物	wù (132) thing	物 物 物 物 物 物
物	
ノ 丬 牛 牛 物	

INDICES

Integrated Chinese I, Part 1 — Character Index
Chronological by Lesson
(Lessons 1-11, including Radicals and Numerals)

*	=	bound form
M	=	Measure word
P	=	Particle
QP	=	Question Particle

Radicals

人／亻	rén	man; person
刀／刂	dāo	knife
力	lì	power
又	yòu	right hand; again
口	kǒu	mouth
囗	wéi	enclose
土	tǔ	earth
夕	xī	sunset
大	dà	big; large
女	nǚ	female; woman
子	zǐ	son; child
寸	cùn	inch
小	xiǎo	little; small
工	gōng	labor; work; craft
幺	yāo	tiny; small
弓	gōng	bow
门／門	mén	door; gate
马／馬	mǎ	horse
心／忄	xīn	heart
戈	gē	dagger-axe
手／扌	shǒu	hand
日	rì	sun
月	yuè	moon
贝／貝	bèi	cowry shell
火／灬	huǒ	fire
木	mù	wood
水／氵	shuǐ	water

田	tián	field
目	mù	eye
示／礻	shì	to show
糸／纟	mì	fine silk
耳	ěr	ear
衣／衤	yī	clothing
言／讠	yán	word
走	zǒu	to walk
足	zú	foot
金／钅	jīn	metal; gold
隹	zhuī	short-tailed bird
雨	yǔ	rain
食／饣	shí	to eat

Numerals

一	yī	one
二	èr	two
三	sān	three
四	sì	four
五	wǔ	five
六	liù	six
七	qī	seven
八	bā	eight
九	jiǔ	nine
十	shí	ten

都		dōu	all; both
医／醫		yī	medicine; doctor

Lesson 3

月		yuè	moon; month
号／號		hào	number
星		xīng	star
期		qī	period (of time)
天		tiān	sky; day
日		rì	day
今		jīn	today; now
年		nián	year
多		duō	many
大		dà	big
岁／歲		suì	age
吃		chī	eat
晚		wǎn	evening; late
饭／飯		fàn	meal
怎		zěn	*how
样／樣		yàng	kind
太		tài	too; extremely
了		le	P
谢／謝		xiè	thank
喜		xǐ	*like; happy
欢／歡		huān	joyful
还／還		hái	still; yet
可		kě	but
们／們		men	*(plural suffix)
点／點		diǎn	dot; o'clock
钟／鐘		zhōng	clock
半		bàn	half
上		shàng	above; top
见／見		jiàn	see
再		zài	again

白		bái	white
现／現		xiàn	now
在		zài	at; in; on
刻		kè	quarter (hour)
明		míng	bright
忙		máng	busy
很		hěn	very
事		shì	affair; matter
为／為		wèi	for
因		yīn	because
同		tóng	same
认／認		rèn	recognize
识／識		shí	recognize

Lesson 4

周／週		zhōu	week
末		mò	end
打		dǎ	hit; strike
球		qiú	ball
看		kàn	see; look
电／電		diàn	electric
视／視		shì	view
唱		chàng	sing
歌		gē	song
跳		tiào	jump
舞		wǔ	dance
听／聽		tīng	listen
音		yīn	sound; music
乐／樂		yuè	music
对／對		duì	correct; toward
时／時		shí	time
候		hòu	wait
书／書		shū	book
影		yǐng	shadow

常		cháng	often	校		xiào	school
去		qù	go	喝		hē	drink
外		wài	outside	茶／茶		chá	tea
客		kè	guest	咖		kā	*coffee
昨		zuó	yesterday	啡		fēi	*coffee
所(所)		suǒ	*so; place	啤		pí	*beer
以		yǐ	with	酒		jiǔ	wine
久		jiǔ	long time	吧		ba	P
错／錯		cuò	wrong; error	要		yào	want
想		xiǎng	think	杯		bēi	cup; glass
觉／覺		jué	feel; reckon	起		qǐ	rise
得		dé	obtain; get	给／給		gěi	give
意		yì	meaning	杯		bēi	cup; glass
思		sī	think	水		shuǐ	water
只		zhǐ	only	玩		wán	play; visit
睡		shuì	sleep	图／圖		tú	drawing
算		suàn	calculate; figure	馆／館		guǎn	accomodations
找		zhǎo	look for; seek	瓶		píng	bottle
别／別		bié	other	聊		liáo	chat
				才		cái	not until; only
				回		huí	return

Lesson 5

呀		ya	P
进／進		jìn	enter
快		kuài	fast; quick
来／來		lái	come
介		jiè	between
绍／紹		shào	carry on
下		xià	below; under
漂		piào	*pretty
亮／亮		liàng	bright
坐		zuò	sit
哪		nǎ / něi	which
工		gōng	labor; work; craft
作		zuò	work; do

Lesson 6

话／話		huà	speech
喂		wèi	Hello!; Hey!
就		jiù	just
位		wèi	M (polite)
午		wǔ	noon
间／間		jiān	M (for rooms)
题／題		tí	topic; question
开／開		kāi	open
会／會		huì	meet
节／節		jié	M (for classes)
课／課		kè	class; lesson

级／級	jí	grade; level
考／考	kǎo	test
试／試	shì	try
后／後	hòu	after
空	kòng	free time
方	fāng	square; side
便	biàn	convenient
到	dào	go to; arrive
办／辦	bàn	manage
公	gōng	public
室	shì	room
行	xíng	all right; O.K.
等	děng	wait
气／氣	qì	air
帮／幫	bāng	help
跟	gēn	with
练／練	liàn	drill
习／習	xí	practice
说／說	shuō	speak
啊	a	P
但	dàn	but
知	zhī	know
道	dào	road; way

Lesson 7

助	zhù	assist
复／復	fù	duplicate
写／寫	xiě	write
慢	màn	slow
教／教	jiāo	teach
笔／筆	bǐ	pen
难／難	nán	difficult; hard
里／裡	lǐ	inside
第	dì	(ordinal prefix)

预／預	yù	prepare
语／語	yǔ	language
法	fǎ	method; way
容	róng	hold; contain; allow
易	yì	easy
懂／懂	dǒng	understand
词／詞	cí	word
汉／漢	hàn	Chinese
平	píng	level; even
早	zǎo	early
夜	yè	night
功	gōng	skill
真(眞)	zhēn	true; real
始	shǐ	begin
念／唸	niàn	read
录／錄	lù	record
帅／帥	shuài	handsome; smart

Lesson 8

篇	piān	M (for articles)
记／記	jì	record
床／牀	chuáng	bed
洗	xǐ	wash
澡	zǎo	bath
边／邊	biān	side
发／發	fā	emit; issue
脑／腦	nǎo	brain
餐	cān	meal
厅／廳	tīng	hall
报／報	bào	newspaper
宿	sù	stay
舍	shè	house
正	zhèng	just; straight
前	qián	front; before

告	gào	tell; inform
诉／訴	sù	tell; relate
已	yǐ	already
经／經	jīng	pass through
封	fēng	M (for letters)
信	xìn	letter
最	zuì	most
近	jìn	near
除	chú	except
专业／專	zhuān	special
业／業	yè	occupation
惯	guàn	be used to
清	qíng	clear; clean
楚	chǔ	clear; neat
步	bù	step
希	xī	hope
望／望	wàng	hope; wish
能	néng	be able
用	yòng	use
笑	xiào	laugh
祝	zhù	wish

Lesson 9

买／買	mǎi	buy
东／東	dōng	east
西	xī	west
售	shòu	sell
货／貨	huò	merchandise
员／員	yuán	personnel
衣	yī	clothing
服	fú	clothing
件	jiàn	M (for items)
衬／襯	chèn	lining
衫	shān	shirt

颜／顏	yán	face; countenance
色	sè	color
黄／黃	huáng	yellow
红／紅	hóng	red
穿	chuān	wear
条／條	tiáo	M (for long objects)
裤／褲	kù	pants
宜	yí	suitable
付	fù	pay
钱／錢	qián	money
共	gòng	altogether
块／塊	kuài	piece; dollar
毛	máo	hair; dime
分	fēn	penny; minute
百	bǎi	hundred
双／雙	shuāng	pair
鞋	xié	shoes
换／換	huàn	change
黑	hēi	black
虽／雖	suī	though; while
然	rán	like that; so
合	hé	suit; agree
适／適	shì	suit; fit

Lesson 10

比	bǐ	compare
雨	yǔ	rain
更	gèng	even more
而	ér	and; in addition
且	qiě	for the time being
暖	nuǎn	warm
约／約	yuē	make an appoint.
园／園	yuán	garden
叶／葉	yè	leaf

像		xiàng	image
海		hǎi	sea
糟		zāo	messy
糕		gāo	cake
又		yòu	again
刚 / 剛		gāng	just now
出		chū	go out
热 / 熱		rè	hot
舒		shū	stretch
夏		xià	summer
凉 / 涼		liáng	cool
春		chūn	spring
冬		dōng	winter
冷		lěng	cold
闷 / 悶		mēn	stuffy
次		cì	M (for occurance)
秋		qiū	autumn; fall
台 / 臺		tái	platform
北		běi	north
湾 / 灣		wān	strait; bay

Lesson 11

寒		hán	cold
假		jià	vacation
飞 / 飛		fēi	fly
机 / 機		jī	machine
票		piào	ticket
场 / 場		chǎng	field
汽		qì	steam
车 / 車		chē	car
或		huò	or
者		zhě	(a suffix)
地		dì	earth
铁 / 鐵		tiě	iron

走		zǒu	walk
路		lù	road; way
站		zhàn	stand; station
绿 / 綠		lù	green
线 / 線		xiàn	line
蓝 / 藍		lán	blue
麻		má	hemp; numb
烦 / 煩		fán	bother
租		zū	rent
送		sòng	deliver
过 / 過		guò	pass
让 / 讓		ràng	let
花 / 花		huā	spend
每		měi	every
速		sù	speed
路		lù	road; way
紧 / 緊		jǐn	tight
自		zì	self
己		jǐ	oneself
新		xīn	new
礼 / 禮		lǐ	gift
物		wù	thing; matter

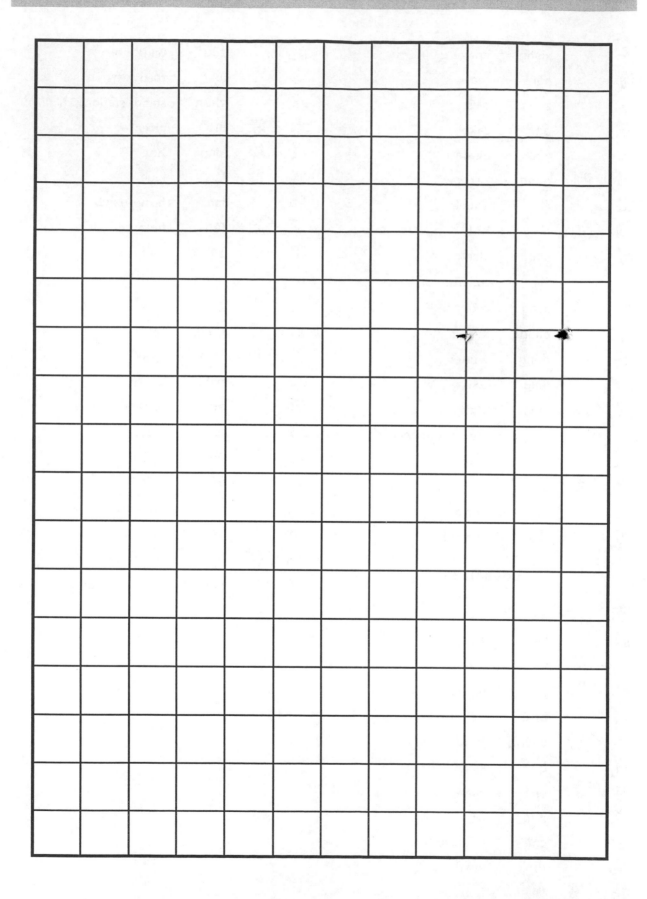

Integrated Chinese I, Part 1 — Character Index
Alphabetical by Pīnyīn

*	=	bound form
M	=	Measure word
P	=	Particle
QP	=	Question Particle

A

| 啊 | a | P | 6.2 |

B

八	bā	eight	Num
爸	bà	dad	2.1
吧	ba	P	5.1
白	bái	white	3.1
百	bǎi	hundred	9.1
半	bàn	half	3.1
办／辦	bàn	manage	6.1
帮／幫	bāng	help	6.2
报／報	bào	newspaper	8.1
杯	bēi	cup; glass	5.1
北	běi	north	10.2
贝／貝	bèi	cowry shell	Rad
笔／筆	bǐ	pen	7.1
比	bǐ	compare	10.1
边／邊	biān	side	8.1
便	biàn	convenient	6.1
别／別	bié	other	4.2
不	bù	not; no	1.2
步	bù	step	8.2

C

才	cái	not until; only	5.2
餐	cān	meal	8.1
茶／茶	chá	tea	5.1
常	cháng	often	4.1
场／場	chǎng	field	11.1
唱	chàng	sing	4.1
车／車	chē	car	11.1
衬／襯	chèn	lining	9.1
吃	chī	eat	3.1
出	chū	go out	10.2
除	chú	except	8.2
楚	chǔ	clear; neat	8.2
穿	chuān	wear	9.1
床／牀	chuáng	bed	8.1
春	chūn	spring	10.2
词／詞	cí	word	7.1
次	cì	M (for occurances)	10.2
寸	cùn	inch	Rad
错／錯	cuò	wrong; error	4.2

D

打	dǎ	hit; strike	4.1
大	dà	big	Rad, 3.1
但	dàn	but	6.2
刀／刂	dāo	knife	Rad
到	dào	arrive	6.1
道	dào	road; way	6.2
得	dé	obtain; get	4.2
的	de	P	2.1
得	děi	must; have to	6.1 (4.2)
等	děng	wait	6.1

弟		dì	younger brother	2.1	高		gāo	tall	2.1
第		dì	(ordinal prefix)	7.1	糕		gāo	cake	10.2
地		dì	earth	11.1	告		gào	tell; inform	8.1
点／點		diǎn	dot; o'clock	3.1	戈		gē	dagger-axe	Rad
电／電		diàn	electric	4.1	哥		gē	older brother	2.2
东／東		dōng	east	9.1	歌		gē	song	4.1
冬		dōng	winter	10.2	个／個		gè	M (general)	2.1
懂		dǒng	understand	7.1	给／給		gěi	give	5.1
都		dōu	all; both	2.2	跟		gēn	with	6.2
对／對		duì	correct; toward	4.1	更		gèng	even more	10.1
多		duō	many	3.1	弓		gōng	bow	Rad

E

工		gōng	craft; work	Rad, 5.1
儿／兒		ér	son; child	2.1	公		gōng	public	6.1
而		ér	and	10.1	功		gōng	skill	7.2
耳		ěr	ear	Rad	共		gòng	altogether	9.1
二		èr	two	Num	馆／館		guǎn	accommodations	5.2

F

惯／慣		guàn	be used to	8.2
发／發		fā	emit; issue	8.1	贵／貴		guì	honorable	1.1
法		fǎ	method; way	7.1	国／國		guó	country	1.2
烦／煩		fán	bother	11.1	过／過		guò	pass	11.2
饭／飯		fàn	meal	3.1
方		fāng	square; side	6.1

H

啡		fēi	*coffee	5.1
飞／飛		fēi	fly	11.1	孩		hái	child	2.1
分		fēn	penny; minute	9.1	还／還		hái	still; yet	3.1
封		fēng	M (for letters)	8.2	海		hǎi	sea	10.1
服		fú	clothing	9.1	寒		hán	cold	11.1
复／復		fù	duplicate	7.1	汉／漢		hàn	Chinese	7.1
付		fù	pay	9.1	好		hǎo	fine; good; OK	1.1
					号／號		hào	number	3.1

G

喝		hē	drink	5.1
					和		hé	and	2.2
					合		hé	suit; agree	9.2
					黑		hēi	black	9.2
刚／剛		gāng	just now	10.2	很		hěn	very	3.2

练／練	liàn	drill	6.2
凉／涼	liáng	cool	10.2
两／兩	liǎng	two; a couple	2.2
亮／亮	liàng	bright	5.1
聊	liáo	chat	5.2
六	liù	six	Num
录／錄	lù	record	7.2
路	lù	road; way	11.2
律	lù	law; rule	2.2
绿／綠	lǜ	green	11.1

M

妈／媽	mā	mom	2.1
麻	má	hemp; numb	11.1
馬／马	mǎ	horse	Rad
吗／嗎	ma	QP	1.2
买／買	mǎi	buy	9.1
慢	màn	slow	7.1
忙	máng	busy	3.2
毛	máo	hair; dime	9.1
么／麼	me	*QP	1.1
没(沒)	méi	(have) not	2.1
美	měi	beautiful	1.2
每	měi	every; each	11.2
妹	mèi	younger sister	2.1
闷／悶	mēn	stuffy	10.2
门／門	mén	door; gate	Rad
们／們	men	*(plural suffix)	3.1
系／纟	mì	fine silk	Rad
名	míng	name	1.2
明	míng	bright	3.2
末	mò	end	4.1
木	mù	wood	Rad
目	mù	eye	Rad

N

哪	nǎ / něi	which	5.1
那	nà / nèi	that	2.1
男	nán	male	2.1
难／難	nán	difficult; hard	7.1
脑／腦	nǎo	brain	8.1
呢	ne	QP	1.1
能	néng	be able	8.2
你	nǐ	you	1.1
年	nián	year	3.1
念／唸	niàn	read	7.2
您	nín	you (polite)	1.1
暖	nuǎn	warm	10.1
女	nǚ	woman; female	Rad, 2.1

P

朋	péng	friend	1.1
啤	pí	*beer	5.1
篇	piān	M (for articles)	8.1
便	pián	*inexpensive	9.1
片	piàn	slice; *film	2.1
漂	piào	*pretty	5.1
票	piào	ticket	11.1
瓶	píng	bottle	5.2
平	píng	level; even	7.2

Q

七	qī	seven	Num
期	qī	period (of time)	3.1
起	qǐ	rise	5.1
气／氣	qì	air	6.1
汽	qì	steam	11.1
前	qián	front; before	8.1

田	tián	(a surname); field	Rad
条／條	tiáo	M (for long objects)	9.1
跳	tiào	jump	4.1
铁／鐵	tiě	iron	11.1
听／聽	tīng	listen	4.1
厅／廳	tīng	hall	8.1
同	tóng	same	3.2
图／圖	tú	drawing	5.2
土	tǔ	earth	Rad

W

外	wài	outside	4.1
湾／灣	wān	strait; bay	10.2
玩	wán	play; visit	5.2
晚	wǎn	evening; late	3.1
王	wáng	(a surname); king	1.1
望／望	wàng	hope; wish	8.2
口	wéi	enclose	Rad
为／為	wèi	for	3.2
位	wèi	M (polite)	6.1
喂	wèi	Hello!; Hey!	6.1
文	wén	script	2.2
问／問	wèn	ask	1.1
我	wǒ	I; me	1.1
五	wǔ	five	Num
舞	wǔ	dance	4.1
午	wǔ	noon	6.1
物	wù	thing; matter	11.2

X

夕	xī	sunset	Rad
希	xī	hope	8.2
西	xī	west	9.1
习／習	xí	practice	6.2

喜	xǐ	like; happy	3.1
洗	xǐ	wash	8.1
下	xià	below; under	5.1
夏	xià	summer	10.2
先	xiān	first	1.1
现／現	xiàn	present	3.2
线／線	xiàn	line	11.1
想	xiǎng	think	4.2
像	xiàng	image	10.1
小	xiǎo	little; small	Rad, 1.1
校	xiào	school	5.1
笑	xiào	laugh	8.2
鞋	xié	shoes	9.2
写／寫	xiě	write	7.1
谢／謝	xiè	thank	3.1
心／忄	xīn	heart	Rad
新	xīn	new	11.2
信	xìn	letter	8.2
星	xīng	star	3.1
行	xíng	all right; O.K.	6.1
姓	xìng	surname	1.1
学／學	xué	study	1.2

Y

呀	ya	P	5.1
言／讠	yán	word	Rad
颜／顏	yán	face; countenance	9.1
样／樣	yàng	kind	3.1
幺	yāo	tiny; small	Rad
要	yào	want	5.1
也	yě	also	1.2
夜	yè	night	7.2
业／業	yè	occupation	8.2
叶／葉	yè	leaf	10.1

一		yī	one	Num
医／醫		yī	doctor; medicine	2.2
衣／衤		yī	clothing	Rad, 9.1
宜		yí	suitable	9.1
以		yǐ	with	4.1
已		yǐ	already	8.1
意		yì	meaning	4.2
易		yì	easy	7.1
因		yīn	because	3.2
音		yīn	sound; music	4.1
英／英		yīng	*England	2.2
影		yǐng	shadow	4.1
用		yòng	use	8.2
友		yǒu	friend	1.1
有		yǒu	have; there is/are	2.1
又		yòu	again	Rad, 10.2
语／語		yǔ	language	7.1
雨		yǔ	rain	Rad, 10.1
预／預		yù	prepare	7.1
员／員		yuán	personnel	9.1
园／園		yuán	garden	10.1
约／約		yuē	make an appoint.	10.1
月		yuè	moon; month	Rad, 3.1
乐／樂		yuè	music	4.1

Z

再	zài	again	3.1
在	zài	at; in; on	3.2
糟	zāo	messy	10.2
早	zǎo	early	7.2
澡	zǎo	bath	8.1

怎		zěn	*how	3.1
站		zhàn	stand; station	11.1
张／張		zhāng	M; (a surname)	2.1
找		zhǎo	look for; seek	4.2
照		zhào	shine	2.1
者		zhě	(a suffix)	11.1
这／這		zhè(i)	this	2.1
真(眞)		zhēn	true; real	7.2
正		zhèng	just; straight	8.1
知		zhī	know	6.2
只		zhǐ	only	4.2
中		zhōng	center; middle	1.2
钟／鐘		zhōng	clock	3.1
周／週		zhōu	week	4.1
助		zhù	assist	7.1
祝		zhù	wish	8.2
专／專		zhuān	special	8.2
隹		zhuī	short-tailed bird	Rad
子		zǐ	son	2.1
字		zì	character	1.1
自		zì	self	11.2
走		zǒu	walk	11.1
租		zū	rent	11.1
足		zú	foot	Rad
最		zuì	most	8.2
昨		zuó	yesterday	4.1
做		zuò	do	2.2
坐		zuò	sit	5.1
作		zuò	work; do	5.1

Integrated Chinese I, Part 1 — Character Index
Arranged by Number of Strokes

*	=	bound form	
M	=	Measure word	
P	=	Particle	
QP	=	Question Particle	

1

一	yī	one	Num

2

八	bā	eight	Num
刀／刂	dāo	knife	Rad
儿／兒	ér	son; child	2.1
二	èr	two	Num
几／幾	jǐ	QP; how many	2.2
九	jiǔ	nine	Num
了	le	P	3.1
力	lì	power; strength	Rad
七	qī	seven	Num
人／亻	rén	man; person	Rad, 1.2
十	shí	ten	Num
又	yòu	again	Rad, 10.2

3

才	cái	not until; only	5.2
寸	cùn	inch	Rad
大	dà	big	Rad, 3.1
飞／飛	fēi	fly	11.1
个／個	gè	M (general)	2.1
工	gōng	craft; work	Rad, 5.1
弓	gōng	bow	Rad
女	nǚ	woman; female	Rad, 2.1
己	jǐ	oneself	11.2
久	jiǔ	long time	4.2

口	kǒu	mouth	Rad
马／馬	mǎ	horse	Rad
么／麼	me	*QP	1.1
门／門	mén	door; gate	Rad
三	sān	three	Num
上	shàng	above; on top	3.1
土	tǔ	earth	Rad
口	wéi	enclose	Rad
夕	xī	sunset	Rad
习／習	xí	practice	6.2
下	xià	below; under	5.1
小	xiǎo	little; small	Rad, 1.1
幺	yāo	tiny; small	Rad
也	yě	also	1.2
已	yǐ	already	8.1
子	zǐ	son	Rad, 2.1

4

办／辦	bàn	manage	6.1
贝／貝	bèi	cowry shell	Rad
比	bǐ	compare	10.1
不	bù	not; no	1.2
车／車	chē	car	11.1
方	fāng	square; side	6.1
分	fēn	penny; minute	9.1
戈	gē	dagger-axe	Rad
公	gōng	public	6.1
火／灬	huǒ	fire	Rad

见／見	jiàn	see	3.1	半		bàn	half	3.1
介	jiè	between	5.1	北		běi	north	10.2
今	jīn	today; now	3.1	边／邊		biān	side	8.1
开／開	kāi	open	6.1	出		chū	go out	10.2
六	liù	six	Num	打		dǎ	hit; strike	4.1
毛	máo	hair; dime	9.1	电／電		diàn	electric	4.1
木	mù	wood	Rad	东／東		dōng	east	9.1
片	piàn	slice; *film	2.1	冬		dōng	winter	10.2
气／氣	qì	air	6.1	对／對		duì	correct; toward	4.1
认／認	rèn	to recognize	3.2	发／發		fā	emit; issue	8.1
日	rì	sun; day	Rad, 3.1	付		fù	pay	9.1
少	shǎo	few	9.1	功		gōng	skill	7.2
什／甚	shén	*what	1.1	汉／漢		hàn	Chinese	7.1
手	shǒu	hand	Rad	号／號		hào	number	3.1
书／書	shū	book	4.1	记／記		jì	record	8.1
双／雙	shuāng	pair	9.2	叫		jiào	call	1.1
水／氵	shuǐ	water	Rad, 5.1	节／節		jié	M (for classes)	6.1
太	tài	too; extremely	3.1	可		kě	but	3.1
天	tiān	sky; day	3.1	乐／樂		lè	happy	5.1 (4.1)
厅／廳	tīng	hall	8.1	礼／禮		lǐ	gift	11.2
王	wáng	(a surname); king	1.1	们／們		men	*(plural suffix)	3.1
为／為	wèi	for	3.2	末		mò	end	4.1
文	wén	script	2.2	目		mù	eye	Rad
五	wǔ	five	Num	平		píng	level; even	7.2
午	wǔ	noon	6.1	且		qiě	for the time being	10.1
心／忄	xīn	heart	Rad	去		qù	go	4.1
以	yǐ	with	4.1	让／讓		ràng	let; allow	11.2
友	yǒu	friend	1.1	生		shēng	be born	1.1
月	yuè	moon; month	3.1	示／礻		shì	to show	Rad
中	zhōng	center; middle	1.2	四		sì	four	Num
专／專	zhuān	special	8.2	他		tā	he	2.1
				台／臺		tái	platform	10.2
				田		tián	(a surname); field	Rad

5

白	bái	white	3.1	外		wài	outside	4.1

写／寫	xiě	write	7.1
业／業	yè	occupation	8.2
叶／葉	yè	leaf	10.1
用	yòng	use	8.2
正	zhèng	just; straight	8.1
只	zhǐ	only	4.2

6

百	bǎi	hundred	9.1
场／場	chǎng	field	11.1
吃	chī	eat	3.1
次	cì	M (for occurances)	10.2
地	dì	earth	11.1
多	duō	many	3.1
而	ér	and	10.1
耳	ěr	ear	Rad
刚／剛	gāng	just now	10.2
共	gòng	altogether	9.1
过／過	guò	pass	11.2
好	hǎo	fine; good; OK	1.1
合	hé	suit; agree	9.2
红／紅	hóng	red	9.1
后／後	hòu	after	6.1
欢／歡	huān	joyful	3.1
回	huí	return	5.2
会／會	huì	meet	6.1
机／機	jī	machine	11.1
级／級	jí	grade; level	6.1
件	jiàn	M (for items)	9.1
考	kǎo	test	6.1
老	lǎo	old	1.2
妈／媽	mā	mom	2.1
吗／嗎	ma	QP	1.2
买／買	mǎi	buy	9.1

忙	máng	busy	3.2
糸／纟	mì	fine silk	Rad
名	míng	name	1.1
那	nà / nèi	that	2.1
年	nián	year	3.1
色	sè	color	9.1
师／師	shī	teacher	1.2
岁／歲	suì	age	3.1
她	tā	she	2.1
同	tóng	same	3.2
问／問	wèn	ask	1.1
西	xī	west	9.1
先	xiān	first	1.1
行	xíng	all right; O.K.	6.1
衣／衤	yī	clothing	Rad, 9.1
因	yīn	because	3.2
有	yǒu	have; there is/are	2.1
约／約	yuē	make an appoint.	10.1
再	zài	again	3.1
在	zài	at; in; on	3.2
早	zǎo	early	7.2
字	zì	character	1.1
自	zì	self	11.2

7

吧	ba	P	5.1
报／報	bào	newspaper	8.1
别／別	bié	other	4.2
步	bù	step	8.2
床／牀	chuáng	bed	8.1
词／詞	cí	word	7.1
但	dàn	but	6.2
弟	dì	younger brother	2.1
饭／飯	fàn	meal	3.1

告		gào	tell; inform	8.1	坐		zuò	sit	5.1
更		gèng	even more	10.1	作		zuò	work; do	5.1
花／花		huā	spend	11.2					
间／間		jiān	M (for rooms)	6.1			**8**		
进／進		jìn	enter	5.1	爸		bà	dad	2.1
快		kuài	fast; quick	5.1	杯		bēi	cup; glass	5.1
块／塊		kuài	piece; dollar	9.1	衬／襯		chèn	lining	9.1
冷		lěng	cold	10.2	到		dào	arrive	6.1
李		lǐ	(a surname); plum	1.1	的		de	P	2.1
里／裡		lǐ	inside	7.1	法		fǎ	method; way	7.1
没(沒)		méi	(have) not	2.1	服		fú	clothing	9.1
每		měi	every; each	11.2	国／國		guó	country	1.2
闷／悶		mēn	stuffy	10.2	和		hé	and	2.2
男		nán	male	2.1	话／話		huà	speech	6.1
你		nǐ	you	1.1	货／貨		huò	merchandise	9.1
汽		qì	steam	11.1	或		huò	or	11.1
识／識		shí	to recognize	3.2	金／钅		jīn	(a surname); gold	Rad
时／時		shí	time	4.1	经／經		jīng	pass through	8.1
诉／訴		sù	tell; relate	8.1	练／練		liàn	drill	6.2
条／條		tiáo	M (for long objects)	9.1	录／錄		lù	record	7.2
听／聽		tīng	listen	4.1	念／唸		niàn	read	7.2
位		wèi	M (polite)	6.1	绍／紹		shào	carry on	5.1
我		wǒ	I; me	1.1	衫		shān	shirt	9.1
希		xī	hope	8.2	始		shǐ	begin	7.2
言／讠		yán	word	Rad	事		shì	matter; affair	3.2
医／醫		yī	doctor; medicine	2.2	视／視		shì	view	4.1
员／員		yuán	personnel	9.1	试／試		shì	try	6.1
园／園		yuán	garden	10.1	所(所)		suǒ	*so; place	4.1
张／張		zhāng	M; (a surname)	2.1	物		wù	thing; matter	11.2
找		zhǎo	look for; seek	4.2	图／圖		tú	drawing	5.2
这／這		zhè(i)	this	2.1	现／現		xiàn	present	3.2
助		zhù	assist	7.1	线／線		xiàn	line	11.1
走		zǒu	walk	Rad, 11.1	姓		xìng	surname	1.1
足		zú	foot	Rad	学／學		xué	study	1.2

夜	yè	night	7.2	
宜	yí	suitable	9.1	
易	yì	easy	7.1	
英／英	yīng	*England	2.2	
雨	yǔ	rain	Rad, 10.1	
周／週	zhōu	week	4.1	
隹	zhuī	short-tailed bird	Rad	

9

帮／幫	bāng	help	6.2
便	biàn	convenient	6.1
茶／茶	chá	tea	5.1
除	chú	except	8.2
穿	chuān	wear	9.1
春	chūn	spring	10.2
点／點	diǎn	dot; o'clock	3.1
封	fēng	M (for letters)	8.2
复／復	fù	duplicate	7.1
给／給	gěi	give	5.1
贵／貴	guì	honorable	1.1
孩	hái	child	2.1
很	hěn	very	3.2
觉／覺	jiào	feel; reckon	4.2
觉／覺	jué	feel; reckon	4.2
看	kàn	see; look	4.1
客	kè	guest	4.1
亮／亮	liàng	bright	5.1
律	lǜ	law; rule	2.2
美	měi	beautiful	1.2
哪	nǎ / něi	which	5.1
便	pián	*inexpensive	9.1
前	qián	front; before	8.1
秋	qiū	autumn; fall	10.2
食／饣	shí	to eat	Rad

是	shì	be	1.2
室	shì	room	6.1
适／適	shì	suit; fit	9.2
帅	shuài	handsome	7.2
说／說	shuō	speak	6.2
思	sī	think	4.2
送	sòng	deliver	11.1
虽／雖	suī	though; while	9.2
洗	xǐ	wash	8.1
信	xìn	letter	8.2
星	xīng	star	3.1
要	yào	want	5.1
音	yīn	sound; music	4.1
语／語	yǔ	language	7.1
怎	zěn	*how	3.1
钟／鐘	zhōng	clock	3.1
祝	zhù	wish	8.2
昨	zuó	yesterday	4.1

10

啊	a	P	6.2
笔／筆	bǐ	pen	7.1
都	dōu	all; both	2.2
烦／煩	fán	bother	11.1
高	gāo	tall	2.1
哥	gē	older brother	2.2
海	hǎi	sea	10.1
换／換	huàn	change	9.2
家	jiā	family; home	2.2
紧／緊	jǐn	tight	11.2
酒	jiǔ	wine	5.1
课／課	kè	class; lesson	6.1
凉／涼	liáng	cool	10.2
难／難	nán	difficult; hard	7.1

脑／腦	nǎo	brain	8.1
能	néng	be able	8.2
瓶	píng	bottle	5.2
起	qǐ	rise	5.1
钱／錢	qián	money	9.1
请／請	qǐng	please; invite	1.1
热／熱	rè	hot	10.2
容	róng	hold; contain	7.1
谁／誰	shéi	who	2.1
速	sù	speed	11.2
铁／鐵	tiě	iron	11.1
夏	xià	summer	10.2
校	xiào	school	5.1
笑	xiào	laugh	8.2
样／樣	yàng	kind	3.1
预／預	yù	prepare	7.1
真(眞)	zhēn	true; real	7.2
租	zū	rent	11.1

11

常	cháng	often	4.1
唱	chàng	sing	4.1
得	dé	obtain; get	4.2
得	děi	must; have to	6.1 (4.2)
第	dì	(ordinal prefix)	7.1
啡	fēi	*coffee	5.1
馆／館	guǎn	accommodations	5.2
惯／慣	guàn	be used to	8.2
黄／黃	huáng	yellow	9.1
假	jià	vacation	11.1
教／敎	jiāo	teach	7.1
聊	liáo	chat	5.2
绿／綠	lù	green	11.1
麻	má	hemp; numb	11.1

您	nín	you (polite)	1.1
啤	pí	*beer	5.1
票	piào	ticket	11.1
清	qīng	clear; clean	8.2
球	qiú	ball	4.1
售	shòu	sell	9.1
宿	sù	stay	8.1
望／望	wàng	hope; wish	8.2
做	zuò	do	2.2

12

道	dào	road; way	6.2
等	děng	wait	6.1
喝	hē	drink	5.1
黑	hēi	black	9.2
就	jiù	just	6.1
裤／褲	kù	pants	9.1
期	qī	period (of time)	3.1
然	rán	like that; so	9.2
舒	shū	stretch	10.2
湾／灣	wān	strait; bay	10.2
晚	wǎn	evening; late	3.1
喂	wèi	Hello!; Hey!	6.1
喜	xǐ	like; happy	3.1
谢／謝	xiè	thank	3.1
最	zuì	most	8.2

13

楚	chǔ	clear; neat	8.2
错／錯	cuò	wrong; error	4.2
跟	gēn	with	6.2
蓝／藍	lán	blue	11.1
路	lù	road; way	11.2
暖	nuǎn	warm	10.1

睡	shuì	sleep	4.2
跳	tiào	jump	4.1
想	xiǎng	think	4.2
新	xīn	new	11.2
意	yì	meaning	4.2
照	zhào	shine	2.1

14

歌	gē	song	4.1
慢	màn	slow	7.1
漂	piào	*pretty	5.1
算	suàn	stay	4.2
舞	wǔ	dance	4.1
像	xiàng	image	10.1

15

懂／懂	dǒng	understand	7.1
篇	piān	M (for articles)	8.1
题／题	tí	topic; question	6.1
鞋	xié	shoes	9.2
颜／颜	yán	face; countenance	9.1
影	yǐng	shadow	4.1

16

餐	cān	meal	8.1
糕	gāo	cake	10.2
澡	zǎo	bath	8.1

17

糟	zāo	messy	10.2

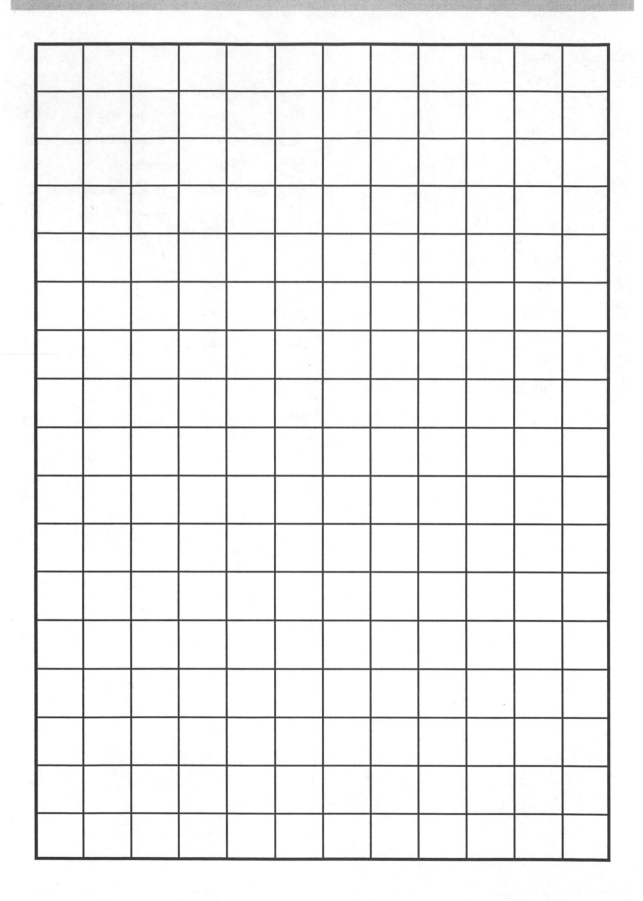